This book is to be returned on or before the date above.
It may be borrowed for a further period if not in demand.

Essex Rich and Strange

The sign of 'The Silent Woman', once at Widford

Essex
Rich and Strange

AN HISTORICAL ENTERTAINMENT

by

RICHARD PUSEY

Drawings by
ROD BROWN

ROBERT HALE · LONDON

© *Richard Pusey 1987*
First published in Great Britain 1987

Robert Hale Limited
Clerkenwell House
Clerkenwell Green
London EC1R 0HT

British Library Cataloguing in Publication Data

Pusey, Richard
 Essex rich and strange.
 1. Essex — Description and travel —
 Guide-books
 I. Title
 914.26'704858   DA670.E7

ISBN 0-7090-3151-3

Photoset in North Wales by
Derek Doyle & Associates, Mold, Clwyd.
Printed in Great Britain by
St Edmundsbury Press Ltd, Bury St Edmunds, Suffolk.
Bound by WBC Bookbinders Limited.

Contents

List of Illustrations

Drawings by Rod Brown

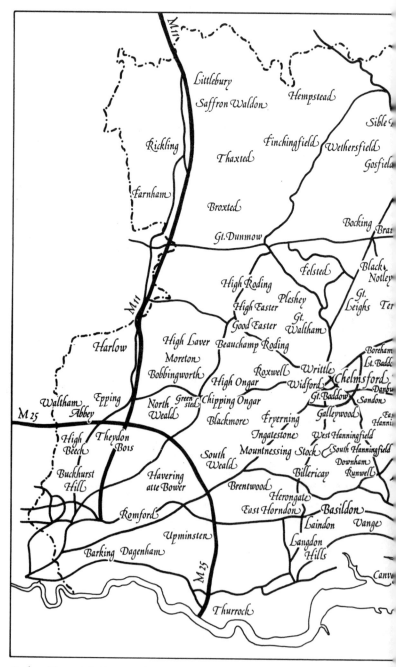

Halstead

Colne

shall
oggeshall

edon

Layer Marney

vitham

Gt.
Totham

raxted

Tolleshunt d'Arcy

Goldhanger

Maldon

Mundon

St. Lawrence

leigh

Latchingdon

Cold Norton

North Fambridge

South
Fambridge

Rochford

n Sea

Southend

River Thames

am
edingham

Langham

Dedham

Colchester

Stanway

Birch

Abberton

Res

Wigborough

Salcott

Virley

The Mouth of the
Blackwater

Osea Island

Bradwell
Juxta Mare

Tillingham

Dengie

Burnham
on Crouch

Mouth of the
Crouch

Foulness

Thorpe
le Soken

Motorway

Major Roads

miles

0 ———— 5

Essex

'... the retriving of these forgotten things from oblivion in some sort resembles the Art of a Conjuror, who makes those walke and appeare that have layen in their grave many hundreds of years: and to represent as it were to the eie, the places, Customes and Fashions, that were of old Times.'

John Aubrey

Preface

This is the second of my books on the county but it differs much from the first in plan and character. The previous book was first and foremost an exploration of the past through the landscape of the present, written as a selective guide for would-be travellers, taking the lanes to some of the lesser-known delights in the Essex countryside. While I hope 'the spirit of place' again comes through in these pages, this volume is much more directly geared to the historical. It aims to celebrate and sample what I have called the phantom scenery of the past, with characters, odd tales, curiosities and houses (some long vanished) brought well into focus. Essex, like every county, can liberally display the rich and the strange: richly varied in associations, strange in stories and lives alien to our time.

I am fully conscious of my debt to so many writers, mainly of old. No researched history can be written otherwise. Burton in his *Anatomy of Melancholy*, a veritable encyclopaedia of quotations, readily confessed: 'That which I have is stolen from others; my page cries out to me, You are a thief.' That acknowledgement I, too, must make in no small measure. Yet the voice is mine, and with Burton also I can hopefully say, 'I have wronged no authors, but given every man his own.'

So much still awaits to be teased out from obscurity and brought to the public eye. As modernity advances, rapidly changing our environment and philosophy of living, the gap between us and our forebears yawns ever wider. This makes us increasingly aware of the need for continuity and roots. So a popular movement grows apace not only to conserve what we can of our visual heritage but to treasure even the echoes of our past. Not to have this wider perspective on the years is to condemn ourselves to a loss of empathy with those who have made their pilgrimage before us.

If this book gives you the entertainment I intend of things rare and unusual, remember, too, that one day we shall also seem just as remote, peculiar and quite outmoded.

1

In Grave Places

'In so busy a land as ours there is no place where the mind can, as it were, turn in upon itself so fully as in the silence and solitude of a village church ... a *visible* silence still as the hourglass ... the sense of man's presence has departed from the walls and oaken seats; the dust here is not the dust of the highway, of the quick footsteps; it is the dust of the past.'

So wrote Richard Jefferies, that lyricist of nature and the landscape, in his essay *Village Churches*. It begs for reading in a country churchyard before we step into the coolness to savour old mortality. 'Oh, do come and see the skulls!' the sexton cried in Jerome's *Three Men in a Boat*, and most of us are very willing to do so.

Enthusiasts for sepulchral architecture, and also for a touch of the bizarre, would do well to visit Boreham. In the side chapel in the chancel of St Andrew's can be seen the tomb of the first three earls of Sussex, namely, Robert, Henry and Thomas Radcliffe. With recumbent effigies, the monument is of alabaster and marble. In their stony silence the three Tudor peers are represented in the plate armour of the time, their swords broken, and at their feet squat monkeys wearing curious hats. The inscriptions are in Latin on black marble and bordered with Egyptian porphyry, each memorial being a concise biography, giving each man's achievements in the service of the Crown. The work of one Richard Stevens of Southwark, the tomb cost £292.12s.8d to make in 1589.

It was Thomas Radcliffe, the third Viscount Fitzwalter, who, in his will of 1583, instructed his executors to commission the building of both the chapel and the tomb.

The Sandys monument in St Mary's, Woodham Ferrers

Although he ordered that he should be buried 'without unnecessary pomp or charges but only having respect to my dignity and state', he set the prodigious limit of £1,500 for his funeral expenses. The family vault holds twelve members of his noble line, among them the fourth, fifth and sixth earls, the last being interred here in 1643. All are wrapped in lead, their names and titles on their breasts.

Wright in his *History of Essex* tells us that some of the effigies have inscriptions on one side and a star and garter on the other. There are coffins, too, in human shape, with eyes, nose, mouth etc, truly a macabre celebration of death.

Only yards away, in the soil outside,

> Each in his narrow Cell for ever laid,
> The rude Forefathers of the Hamlet sleep.

'Oblivion,' Sir Thomas Browne wrote in his *Urn Burial*, 'is not to be hired: the greater part must be content to be as though they had never been, to be found in the register of God, not in the record of man.' However, from parish registers we can often learn a little of those who made their exits without a brass or headstone. Boreham's registers are unusually rich in this respect.

Thus, in 1562 Betteris Apreys or ap Rice, 'laundress to Queen Marie', was laid to rest, having served Mary Tudor when she lived as a closely watched princess at New Hall during the reign of Edward VI. Three entries record parishioners whose days were long in the land: for 1573, Christian Norel, widower, 108 years old; in 1585, Henrie Wolmer, 100 years old; and in 1600, John Read, another centenarian. Among those who met their end through accident there is John Francis, 'slayne with a deer' in 1613, and Nicholas Skinner who, in 1741, 'dyed by a fall from the Battlements at New-hall'. Several children drowned in ponds and one in a gravel pit.

But perhaps the most arresting of the entries is that of Mother Haven who 'suffered at Boreham for witchcraft' and was buried on 29 July 1593. A capital letter 'H' precedes her name, which may signify the Latin '*humo*', which means to hide, cover up or bury. Her interment would have been in unconsecrated ground. Alternatively, the letter could simply mean 'hanged'. Apart from her appearance in the parish book, nothing else seems to be known of this unfortunate woman.

For the connoisseur of matters mortuary, the church at Hempstead has no small fascination with its vault and memorials of the Harveys. And the village has the added 'draw' of being the birthplace of Dick Turpin, son of the landlord at the Bell, now known as the Rose and Crown. As at Boreham, the church is dedicated to St Andrew.

The most famous of the deceased here is William Harvey, who discovered the *modus operandi* for the circulation of the blood. He is commemorated with a striking bust, the face reputed to be a true likeness taken from a death-mask. He died at the age of eighty in 1657, in Roehampton, at the house of his brother Eliab, a wealthy merchant. The doctor was brought to lie at Hempstead, where the family had its seat. The body was carried in solemn procession from London by fellow members of the College of Physicians.

John Aubrey knew him well, and his account of Dr Harvey is one of the most compelling of the *Brief Lives*. Aubrey was at the funeral and helped to carry the body into the vault. There it remained for over two centuries while the chamber was gradually filled with over forty succeeding members of the family. Writing in 1861, Coller noted an odd report in his *People's History of Essex*: 'Not long since the sexton was stated to be in the habit of converting the vault into a showroom and rattling the bones of the great philosopher in his coffin for the entertainment of his audience. The publication of the fact put an end to this indignity to the illustrious dead; and there is some hope of the monument being restored, or the coffin transferred to some more worthy resting place.' This was finally done in 1883, the remains being moved to the chapel above and placed in a white sarcophagus given by the Royal College of Physicians. The college had been endowed with a superb library by Harvey, and a further act of their generosity was to later rebuild the church tower which had fallen in 1882. Provided for from a memorial fund, its renewal took three decades to achieve until its completion in 1961.

The second most distinguished member of the family to be buried here was Sir Eliab Harvey, a direct descendant of William's brother. Sir Eliab, Admiral of the Blue and three times MP for the county, commanded the ninety-eight gun *Fighting Téméraire* at Trafalgar.

In one of her charming books, *The Essex Village in Days Gone By*, Miss Eliza Vaughan gave a first-hand description of the Harvey vault, although I very much doubt if access to it is so readily given today:

It can still be seen by any who wish to do so, and, though a grim place, it is well worth a visit. Access is gained from the outside of the chancel wall: a large trap door covering the flight of old stone steps which lead downwards to the vault. At the base of the steps a strange sight meets the eye, for lying scattered about in somewhat a state of confusion are leaden coffins of every size, and made in the shape of the human form, all containing the bones of succeeding generations of the Harveys, from the 17th to the 19th centuries. To add to the weird effect, the head of each coffin has graven upon it the features of a face, evidently the likeness of the person whose body is inside the lead. They are not gruesome, but life-like and full of character. Old Eliab, the founder of the Hempstead family, is portrayed there: and many ladies' and little children's faces of long bygone days look as if one might have known them and met them in the village street. I can remember seeing in my youth the features of the great doctor depicted on his coffin before the College of Physicians removed it, and shut it up in the modern marble tomb in the Harvey Chapel above.

Miss Vaughan goes on to describe the coffin of the naval hero, Sir Eliab: '... one of the few ordinary shaped coffins of a later period. It is large, and covered with blue velvet, which still retains its beautiful colour, and ornamented with silver fittings.' As child she had seen, too, the scarlet velvet-draped coffin of Captain Edward Harvey, eldest son of Sir Eliab, who had fallen during the Peninsular War in 1812. To his great distress, which must have fed his violent temperament, the old man lived to see each of his three boys die, one as a youngster, while his six daughters and his wife survived him. He passed into the darkness of the crypt in 1830.

In addition to William Harvey, another major figure in the sciences lies in an Essex churchyard. This is John Ray, naturalist and a founder of modern botany. Born in Black Notley in 1628, the son of the village blacksmith, he went to the grammar school in Braintree and then on to Catherine Hall and Trinity at Cambridge, where he secured an MA. With his friend and one-time pupil Frances Willoughby, he travelled much in Britain and on the Continent in search of rare plants. Returning from abroad, he was made a Fellow of the Royal Society. His greatest work was his three-volume

History of Plants which covered 11,000 species. In his later years he gave up his residence in Cambridge and settled once more in Black Notley, in his mother's house, 'Dewlands', which stood until destroyed by fire in 1900.

Among Ray's works were *Three Physico-theological Discourses Concerning the Chaos, Deluge, and Dissolution of the World*, and the book long considered his masterpiece, *The Wisdom of God Manifested in the Works of the Creation*.

In both their titles and contents they exhibit a religious perspective to his close study of the natural world. (He had once been in Holy Orders.) This is a marked characteristic of scientific enquiry prior to the nineteenth century, when knowledge became fully secularized, and we shall meet with it again in the life of Dr Derham of Upminster.

John Ray died in 1706, aged seventy-eight. His tomb, a large, square-pedestalled monument, stands near the porch of the parish church, St Peter and St Paul. The long, Latin inscription has appeared in several translations, of which I find the most appealing done in verse. It includes these lines of praise:

> Hid in this narrow tomb, this marble span,
> Lies all that death could snatch from this great man;
> His body moulders in its native clay,
> While o'er wide worlds his works their beams display,
> As bright and everlasting as the day ...
> Like Solomon, (and Solomon alone,
> We as a greater king of knowledge own)
> Our modern sage dark nature's secrets read,
> From the tall cedar to the hyssop's bed;
> From the unwieldest beast of land or deep
> To the least insect that has power to creep ...
> A great descent lent nothing to his fame,
> Virtue, not birth, distinguished his high name ...
> England's blest church engrossed his zealous care,
> A truth his dying accents did declare.
> Thus lost he in retirement his great breath – .
> Thus died he living who thus lives in death –
> Thus has heaven called his age's glory home
> And the bright wonder of the age to come.

Ray's tomb was erected by a bishop of London. Further south, at Woodham Ferrers, there is another with closer episcopal connections. This is the lovely monument in St Mary's to Cecilie Sandys, second wife of Edwin Sandys, Archbishop of York from 1577 to 1588. His life was not without dramatic incident, while Cecilie came near to being murdered.

Sandys was not an Essex man – he was born in the Lake District – but it seems the family had held the chief manor in Woodham Ferrers from the beginning of the sixteenth century. The Archbishop is reputed to have built the moated Hall, part of which remains. At Cambridge, where he was Vice-Chancellor, he came out in support of Lady Jane Grey, in 1553, for which he was imprisoned. Managing to escape, he took refuge at Woodham, but within hours, acting on a warning, he fled to the coast and hence to Antwerp and then Strasbourg. Later he returned in favour to England, becoming Bishop of Worcester, then of London, and finally appointed to the See of York. For several years he was the victim of a blackmail, at first endured in silence, but which he brought into the open in 1583, when he was cleared.

The attempt on the life of Cecilie Sandys was made in the autumn of 1594. The case can be found in court records for that year. She was a life tenant of Edwins Hall, known then as Edwards Hall, and was there with a son and her servants when it was attacked by fourteen men, armed and with 'guns charged with shot and powder'. They broke in and in the assaults that followed wounded several of the occupants. Later, four of the mob, most of them not local men, were apprehended, tried and imprisoned. The ringleader, explicitly charged with inciting them to murder, apparently had a lease on part of the Hall, and a previous dispute with its distinguished tenant seems to have fired the affair.

The monument to Cecilie Sandys, with its sculptured arbour of roses, took the eye of Pevsner as 'exceptional and enchanting'. It stands behind the communion rails and shows her kneeling between two pillars. Above her is a phoenix, and the figure of Father Time, hourglass in hand, is to her left. Formerly there was a figure of Death on the right. This impressive memorial was erected by her eldest son, Sir

Samuel Sandys. It records the burial of four of her other sons here, one of whom, Miles, had been with her on that frightening night in 1594.

Cecilie's inscription tells us: 'She lived a pure maid twenty-four years; a chaste and loving wife twenty-nine years; a true widow twenty-two years to hir last ... a true mirror of a Christian matron she departed this life, constant in Christian faith, February 5th 1610, at the rising of the sun.'

So far we have been in the presence of Names, with figures who have left their mark upon the national scene. It is time to come to a few whose lives and reputations were of more local stature.

Many readers will know the charm of Finchingfield, justly renowned for its setting: a picture-postcard village, especially out of season, which has few equals in East Anglia. And they will know, as well, the church, with its squat tower and curious cupola rising above the houses on the hill, flanked by the old guildhall which leads into the churchyard and by the pub which replaced the Green Man, lost by fire in 1905. But few, I should think, have heard of the very odd tale which lies behind a cryptic line here in an epitaph: 'Here lies William Kempe Esq, pious, just, hospitable, master of himself so much, that what others scarce do by force and penalties, he did by a voluntary constancy hold his peace seven years. Who was interred June tenth, 1628, aged seventy-three ...'

Kempe lived at Spains Hall, one of the three with this name in Essex: a fine Elizabethan house later owned by the Ruggles-Brise family who continue to live there today. He was born in 1555 and was over thirty when he married Phillippa Gunter, who gave him his one and only child, a daughter christened Jane. He would have remained little more than a name were it not for his extraordinary decision in 1618. (That event, with added colouring, passed into the local folklore, and can be found as well in the writing of a near contemporary of Kempe. This was George Firman who became the pastor of Shalford until he joined the ranks of the ejected ministers in 1662.)

The kernel of the story is that one day in the summer of

1618, in a sudden, unjust rage of jealousy and suspicion, William rounded on his wife, accusing her of infidelity. He quickly regretted his act, but so deep and wounding was his shame that his impetuosity passed to another extreme. He vowed never to allow another word to pass his lips. For seven years he held his silence, which he persisted in even after the death of Phillippa in 1623. Tradition has it that for each of those years he dug for commemoration a 'stew' or pond on his estate. One of these remains, and there are traces of others. But it is now known from a map prepared for Kempe in 1618 that all seven were there by that date.

It is Firmin, in his *Brief Vindication* of the Puritan divine Stephen Marshall, who gives the conclusion to the story. In 1625 the minister of Finchingfield died, and William Kempe, who had the right of benefice, wrote 'that no man should have it but Mr Marshall'. And it was Marshall who was instrumental in persuading the squire to break his long silence. In the words of Firmin: 'Mr Marshall, when he came to the Living, soon Wrought upon his Patron to lay by his Pen and Converse with Men by his Tongue; he brought him to Public Worship, hundreds of Spectators wondering to see him come to church.'

Three years later Kempe's life came to an abrupt end with a fit and he was laid into the greater silence by the side of his wife. It was his nephew who provided the memorial.

A loyal pastor in the Great Rebellion was Simon Lynch of Runwell. He lies in the old priory church at Blackmore, and a grey marble partially tells us why: 'Here lyeth the body of Simon Lynch, Rector of Runwell, who, for fearing God and the king, was sequestered, prosecuted and persecuted, to the day of his death, by Gog and Magog ... He died the nineteenth of June 1660, aged 60 years.' (Gog and Magog were synonymous with tyranny. In the Book of Revelations they stand for all the enemies of the Kingdom of God, and Gog became identified with the Antichrist.)

Lynch was instituted at Runwell in 1629 by a namesake, also Simon and presumably his father who held the living at North Weald. After the outbreak of the Civil War, he was deprived of the living in favour of 'a godly, preaching minister', the usual expression for one approved by the

Puritans. Despite the words on his tombstone, however, he does not seem to have fared too badly, for he retained the curacy while being the incumbent at Blackmore, and his family had a fifth of the tithes at Runwell until his death. One of the family wrote of him: he 'rode every Sunday from North Weale his father's house where he sojourned to Blackmore to supply his cure and officiate, which was seven miles and as bad a road as a man could ride, and in all weathers for some years ... not for profit but for conscience sake'. He lived in time to see the Restoration but, 'Just as he was going to receive and take possession of his parsonage [at Runwell] he made his exit.' His memorial stone was at his request, and the inscription was in his will.

On a monument in the Church of St Nicholas at Witham there is another inscription which much takes my fancy, especially for its lengthy coda. Translated, it is to a Robert Barwell, Gent, who died in 1697 of a sudden stroke of apoplexy. His age was forty-four, whereas that of his parents 'together amounted to more than one hundred and sixty years'. The final lines both lament and offer consolation for early departure:

> Whilst the parent lives to an uncommon age,
> Behold the offspring is early taken off:
> How few number many years? Of what avail is medicine?
> Of what benefit the now conquered skill of Galen! ...
> But why all this sorrow! Whence the cause of all this
>   lamentation!
> When the fate of those whom a long series of illness torments
>   Is much worse than this man's.
>   He descends with ease into his grave;
> He can scarcely be said to die, but rather to depart from life.

Should you want two really telling recitals of misfortune, you must go to Great Waltham. You will find them in the nave of the lovely parish church. Both testify to bravery and ironic fate writ large. One I have given in Chapter 4. The other is to Peter Curvengen. His monument was erected by his wife.

Near this place lyeth the body of Peter Curvengen, merchant.

He was sent in his youth to the East Indies, where, attaining a thorough knowledge of the India trade in all its branches, he acquired a plentiful fortune, and with all, what is more valuable, the universal character of a man of great honour and honesty, of inviolable faith and integrity, which virtues he adorned with uncommon affability and politeness. Preparing, after a twenty-five years absence, to return to his native country, he unfortunately fell into the hands of Cannajee Angria, admiral to the Sou Raja, then at war with the English, at Bombay, and remained in a miserable captivity five years; during which time, with an unparalleled patience, generosity, and greatness of mind, he continued not only comforting, assisting, and supporting his fellow-sufferers, but even refusing his own deliverance, without that of his companions in misery. At last, having freed himself and the rest by his own industry and management, he embarked for England in hopes of sitting down in quiet, and enjoying the fruits of his labours. But see the uncertainty of all things below! Just before his landing, a violent fit of the cramp seizing his thigh and bursting the vein, though the effects were hardly discernible, yet was he forced, soon after his arrival in London, to have his thigh first laid open, and then cut off almost close to his body. Scarcely ever was the like operation performed! Never any undergone with more resolution and firmness, without so much as a groan, or the least motion to express his anguish. He outlived this operation twelve days, when the wound, bleeding afresh, he resigned his last breath, with a surprising sedateness and unconcern at leaving this world, being fully persuaded he was going to exchange his perishable for everlasting riches. He died June 26th, 1729, in the 47th year of his age.

It is rare to find a moment of black comedy in the literature on tombs, so I was delighted to find a classic instance in the 'Notes and Queries' of the *Essex Review* for January 1932. The writer, in giving an account of family pews and burial rights in the ground below, referred to the vault of the Snells at Bocking, 'one of the many burrowed into the space beneath St Mary's Church like a miniature catacomb'. He then proceeds with gusto to tell the following:

A thrilling moment occurred in Bocking Church when the ancient timbers gave way one Sunday morning, and the tall form of the late John English Tabor suddenly disappeared from behind the little red curtain and glass rail which surrounds the Squire's pew. The death-watch beetle had been at its full work, and the massive squire was precipitated, with all his eighteen stone, on top of seven vast lead coffins containing a varied assortment of Snells. The least concerned of anyone in the sacred building was our squire. Accustomed from his youth up to taking a toss from off those tall hunters which he regularly bestrode, old John regarded his tumble as all in the day's work. Rising from the ruins with his hymn-book still grasped in his left hand, he casually asked a bystander to pick up his hat out of the ditch, and resumed his singing – far less perturbed than the spluttering choristers whom the organist was endeavouring to pull together by a full blast from the Horn, the Vox Humana and the Diapason.

Nearly all of these tales from the crypt have been of memorable worthies, so I will conclude with two unknowns who share a spot which more than once has been 'by time's fell hand defaced'.

At Rivenhall two sisters lay beneath a stone close to the south side of the steeple. They were long remembered in the parish for a donation, a legacy of £4 per annum to purchase herrings for the poor, a not unusual charity in those times. For many years the fish were doled out every Friday throughout Lent. To this end, a small house was erected over the grave. But this, too, went into oblivion, crushed when part of the church tower fell upon it. Later, only yards away a Roman villa with a tessellated pavement was unearthed along with coins of two emperors.

2

Old 'Flemings'

Houses which have declined in state, relics of their former selves, have a particular fascination. They stand as ciphers in the landscape.

One such is Flemings in the parish of Runwell. Hidden well away on Brock Hill behind Foxearth Wood, it is one of the many in Essex which have known grander times. Once possessed by knightly families, the fine mansion has largely gone, leaving but a remnant of itself in the farmhouse there today. Little is known of its ancient occupants as flesh and blood individuals. They are but shadows. So my brief telling to begin with is inevitably a recital of names. There is small hope now that one day they will be more.

The house takes its name from the Fleming family who held the property over six centuries ago. The first on record is Robert Fleming, here with his wife Alice in 1324. In that year he presented to the living of the parish church one Robert de Rudeham (the first known rector, Rudulphus, took office in 1181), and the family continued to hold the right of benefice for more than one hundred years. Robert's successors had the manor through the reign of Edward III and the following six kings. In that of King Edward IV, Sir Thomas Fleming possessed it. When he died, in 1464, his son John, then fifteen years old, inherited. He held the estate from St Paul's Cathedral, which had owned all the land in Runwell from before the Conquest. There are no memorials in the parish church which bear the name of Fleming, but sepulchral slabs of the thirteenth century, some of them built into the fabric, must have marked the graves of some of the family.

Old 'Flemings' today

John Fleming died without children. The male line coming to an end, his co-heirs were his sisters. One of these, Anne, married a Thomas Copdowe. Their daughter Elizabeth married Edward Sulyard or Suliard, and in this way the estate passed to that family.

Of the Suliards a good deal more is known. They were a Suffolk family who came from Eye. The first who rose to more than local importance was Sir John Suliard who, in 1485, at the very beginning of the Tudor period, became a Justice of the King's Bench. Twice married, by his first wife he had Edward, his heir. His second wife gave him a son and three daughters. In the Suffolk village of Wetherden, Sir John was responsible for the south aisle of the parish church.

Edward Suliard also married twice. By his first marriage he had four sons. Of these William, later knighted, was his heir. The second wife, Anne, gave him a son and a daughter, Eustace and Mary.

Away in the church at High Laver there is a brass which has been dated around 1520. It bears miniature figures of Edward and his first wife, and Wright in his *History of Essex* recorded it as follows: 'Under the effigy of a man and a woman, on a brass plate, in old English characters, with four sons and one daughter:

> Here lieth in grave under this marbyl hande,
> Of John Copto, esquier, the dought and heyre by right,
> Myrabyll, late wife of Edward Sulyard,
> Coosyn and heir of Thomas Flemmyng, knyght,
> Whoise vtue, worth, and womanly delite,
> Remayne shall in Esex in pptuall memorie,
> Sith deth hathe her rafte owt of the psent light.

Sir William Suliard died without issue, and his estate in the main went to a cousin, a descendant of Judge Suliard on his mother's side. But it was Eustace who inherited Flemings.

When Eustace died in 1546, six years after his father, he was buried in Runwell church, where he and his wife Margaret are commemorated by brasses. She came from Little Birch and had wed three times. By her first husband she had a girl, Dorothy. Her second marriage, to Eustace, produced five daughters and Edward, the next heir to Flemings. All are mentioned in her will, of which I give more below. After the death of Eustace she married William Ayloffe of Braxted Lodge. They had no children, although William had several by a previous marriage. He died in 1569. There is some confusion, it would seem, over the recording of her death. Her memorial gives in words the year 1586, in the 'twenteth yere of Our Soveraigne Ladye Queene Elizabeth'. But that year was in fact 1578. Margaret's will is dated July 1579, witnessed seven years later, and proved the following year, 1587.

Her son Edward, who received a knighthood, died in 1610. Of his three children Sir Thomas passed away in 1634. His son, another Edward, died a bachelor in 1692, aged seventy-two. He is remembered by an inscription in the parish church which ends with the words 'the last of his house and of his family'.

And so the line of the Suliards at Runwell faded out. But the main branch in Suffolk flourished until 1811, at Haughley Park, a royal manor they had held from 1538. Their fine early seventeenth-century house is still there. Although devastated by fire in 1961, it was authentically restored and landscaped.

Flemings passed to two nieces. Anne married Charles Parker, the son of a well-known London physician. She is buried with him and their son Charles in the church, their interment marked by a black marble memorial on the floor. The other niece, Dorothy, had a girl who by her marriage to John Tyrell of Billericay brought Flemings into the hands of that distinguished family.

But the Tyrell connection was already established, as can be seen from the will of Margaret Ayloffe. She had purchased land in the district from Sir Henry Tyrell. This included Sudburys, and the name survives as a local farm and road name. Her sister Jane was wed to Thomas Tyrell, son and heir of Sir Henry, and they had a son called Edward.

Margaret's will abounds in informative detail. From it we know that several of her daughters were married. One of them, Margaret, had made a particularly good match, for her husband was Thomas D'Arcy, whose family was one of the most outstanding in the county. Another, Dorothy, had married Antony Maxey of Bradwell juxta Coggeshall. His family name endures there still in Maxeys Spring, marked on the six-inch Ordnance Survey map. Margaret Ayloffe obviously had a special affection for him, writing of him as 'my well-beloved and trusty friend'. Her daughter Anne was married to John Glascocke of Roxwell, and a fourth, Bridget, was also wed.

Among Margaret's bequests to her kith and kin are numerous valuables, and these give some insight into the style in which they lived at Flemings in the Elizabethan age. They included a tablet of gold with a face made with a stone; a tablet set with a 'unicorn' horn having a ruby and diamond; a ring with a turquoise engraved with a face; another bearing a sapphire; and one of gold. She left much silver and gilt. Among these items were the following: a ewer of silver and a basin of the same, weighing 83 ounces; six of her silver plates and four silver spoons; several gilt bowls and a silver tankard; and to her sister Jane 'my little gilt salt, my silver salt with a cover and my little pepperbox'. Also bequeathed was the tester or overhang to her bed, probably a four-poster, 'paned or guarded with purple velvet'. Gifts of money to individuals amounted to around £100, not including the sums left for the administration of her will and for the funeral. £6.13s.4d. was to be set aside annually 'toward finding one scholar in the University of Cambridge'. The poor of the district and her servants were not forgotten. The latter included her gardener, a servant who was also her virginal player, and a French butler.

Had Margaret Ayloffe lived some decades earlier, in Catholic times, no doubt she would have left money for Masses to be said for the repose of her soul. Instead, her executors were to 'procure 20 sermons to be preached in Runwell church by some discreet and well-learned preacher, to have 6s.8d for every sermon, and at every sermon 5s to the poor of Runwell'.

But interesting though this and the family trees may be, the mansion of Flemings and its fate must be of greater appeal for most. In its heyday it was an impressive place, to judge from accounts of its scale and setting. Coller, writing in 1861, gives this from a writer of the previous century:

Fifty spacious rooms and a large chapel (till a fire consumed about thirty of them at the time of Mr Parker's possessing it) was not more than half the original house. Adjoining to the chapel was a burial ground, as appears from the many bones, skulls and parts of coffins that have been frequently disturbed from their place of interment by the diligent plough. There were likewise belonging to it an extensive park, a large warren, fine canals, delightful woods, and in short everything conducive to render it a most elegant and pleasing country seat. But what will appear almost incredible to those who have formed their notions of Essex by riding only from London to Harwich, this house commands a view over parts of this county and Kent, including more than thirty parish churches.

To this quotation Coller added: 'Arched roofs and antique carvings and paintings attest to its magnificence and antiquity. But John Tyrell Esq of Hatfield despoiled the venerable mansion of many fine paintings on glass.' Among the furnishings were portraits of the Sybils and the Caesars. Then, quoting from another source, un-named, he concluded: 'It is indeed difficult to account how fashion should have so far overcome taste as to compel the latter to abandon Flymyngs Hall to neglect and dilapidation.'

The precise year of the fire seems unknown but with the Parkers in residence it must have occurred in the early years of the eighteenth century. The house is one of several exceptional mansions in the area which have regrettably vanished, among them Fremnells, demolished and under Hanningfield Reservoir since 1953, Downham Hall, the seat of the de Beauvoir family, and New Peverell Hall at Tanfield Toy in West Hanningfield, drawn on a Walker map of 1611. Also under the southern end of the reservoir lie the foundations of Giffords, an attractive sixteenth-century farmhouse.

The farmhouse of Flemings is all that remains of the great house which, from what is left, has been dated to around 1600. Norden's map of the county (1594) shows it to the south of the parish church, whereas the present building lies to the north. The map could be in error, but that there was a house long before 1600 is clear from the will of Margaret

Ayloffe, and established beyond all doubt by the earlier will of Eustace Suliard. It contains, among other items, a description not only of the family plate but of the state bed and the armoury.

In 1896 there was a reference in the *Essex Review* to 'a very elaborately panelled oak chimneypiece, occupying the whole width and height of the chimney breast', given as being on the first floor. A mutilated shield in a light on the ground floor is also mentioned, bearing the arms of the Suliards surrounded by a wreath in painted glass. Of particular merit today is a room which was on a corner of the original building, with a bay window of five lights, rising two floors in height and having a gable with obelisks. Some of the timbers in this wing have been called church-like in their construction. The chimney-stack with diagonal shafts has been expertly renewed.

As I was completing this chapter, I was invited to Flemings by Mr Alan Jessup, who purchased both the house and the farm early in 1986. I was delighted with what I saw.

The house is indeed in an enviable setting. The day was flooded with autumnal colour which brought out the mellow tints of brick and stone. The proud owner is a man who well knows what he is about, restoring Flemings with a finely judged taste and expertise, committed to giving the house a character which will continue to speak authentically of its past. I am sure that when he has finished his labours it will truly evoke the nobility of what has gone.

I was taken quite unawares by what remains. Among the appealing things here are a multitude of ancient beams and a fine old doorway, which has been re-sited. The shield on glass survives, and of particular merit is the oak chimney-piece upstairs, Jacobean and panelled in the Renaissance style with architectural motifs. The enemy is rising damp, as in all houses suffering from the years. That is being put to rights, and a staircase in the Elizabethan style should be in place by the time these comments are in print.

At right angles to the house, facing north, there is a subsidiary building. Cottage-like and of just one storey, part of this has old beams and windows which give it every appearance of having once been the chapel, to which a bakehouse has later been attached. Having been given full liberty to photograph and wander, it was with reluctance when I finally drove away.

The *Guide* to the archives of the Essex Record Office does not list any old documents relating to Flemings, unlike nearby Runwell Hall which is well represented. But the index of wills held at Chelmsford may well show wills other than the two I have mentioned here. The parish registers lodged with the ERO may also repay a search for further details on the occupants of the house who have made their entrances and exits down the years.

3

Downham and Bygone 'Fremnells'

In the last chapter I alluded in passing to two notable old mansions in Downham, a parish which adjoins that of Runwell on its western boundary. And although both properties have gone, Downham is well worth a visit on several counts, for not only is it one of those places in which you can catch the resonances of the past but it offers, too, the unexpected enjoyment in this part of Essex of 'bold undulations'.

Away from the eastern end of the scattered village, the parish church, dedicated to St Margaret, stands isolated in a commanding position. In 1861 it was described as 'half concealed amongst groups of venerable trees on a noble hill'. This is not its appearance now, the elms having gone, but this has left the church even more open in the landscape. It is visible for miles around, and the distant view from the church is one of the finest panoramas in Essex.

Apart from the brick and battlemented tower, dating from around 1500, and the earlier, timbered porch, the body of the church was rebuilt in 1871, although several original windows were retained. In our own time the church was gutted by an act of juvenile arson but has now been fully renovated in its former style.

Pevsner noted 'handsome minor epitaphs of C18 and early C19 under the tower' but he gave no further details. Other, older sources, however, are more informative about the antiquities. Wright mentions the inscription to 'Good Sir Henry Terrell' (Tyrell) who died in the year of the Armada. *Kelly's Directories* list a number of memorials, including the above to Sir Henry and his wife; one to Joyce, wife of John

St Margaret's, Downham

Tyrell, 1594; and another to Benjamin Disbrowe of 1707 and his wife Sarah, 1692. Arthur Mee in his book on Essex refers to a brass inscription in French 'saved from the old church'. He also writes of fragments of fourteenth-century stained glass showing golden crowns.

So much for some bare facts about the church, but as with so many of our old churches its days have not been without colour, including a few scandals in remoter times.

In 1596 the churchwardens reported, no doubt with much amazement, one Joan Towler of the parish who 'came into our church in man's attire in the service time'. Another parishioner, two decades earlier, Charles Bundocke, was 'suspected to be an evil and lewd provoker of women to lewdness and whoredom with him'. Strong stuff indeed. The outcome of this accusation is not known. Perhaps its very fierceness was enough to deter.

Then there was the troublesome William Drywood, the rector from 1574 to 1608. In 1580 he was charged at Quarter Sessions with illegal gambling on New Year's Day as well as on other occasions, playing at dice and cards, and was further indicted as a disturber of the peace, calling his parishioners 'boors, steers, notorious liars and drunken thieves'. In the same year he had to face a further bevy of complaints. The list was long: neglecting the repair of the chancel, failing to provide sermons (only six being given in $2\frac{1}{2}$ years), denying Communion to four women who had gone to church to give thanks for their newly born children, keeping animals in the churchyard, which led to 'the graves rooted up', and likening his congregation to hogs and dogs. He denied all the charges and said of the sermons that there had been but one omission. Clearly, he was not only unpopular with his flock but marked down by the Puritan party as a 'gamester' and a non-preaching parson. (Although evangelical nonconformity had yet to become a major force in the politics of the Church, this was an age when the centre of gravity was swinging decisively from the altar to the pulpit.) Just a few years before these charges Drywood's wife, too, was under the shadow, being labelled 'an unquiet woman'. But for all this, the parson held the living for thirty-four years!

The foremost manor in the parish was that of Downham Hall, anciently held by the de Veres, earls of Oxford. Having known a succession of owners, it was purchased in 1714 by Osmond Beauvoir, who came from Hackney. He became a Sheriff of Essex in 1742.

The de Beauvoir family was here until well into the next century. Judging from the representation of the Hall on the

Chapman & André map of 1777, it was a fine residence, surrounded by gardens of formal design. One member of the family, Peter de Beauvoir, was the rector of Downham for the remarkable length of sixty-one years: from 1760 to 1821. The name endures in that of the village pub, the De Beauvoir Arms, known locally as 'the Beavers'. It has been called that at least since 1848, when the victualler was also a carpenter. A nearby farm also carries the distinguished name.

By the middle of the last century the mansion was only a remnant, 'having been demolished some time ago'. It was sited in a hollow just yards to the south-east of the church, where Downham Hall farmhouse now stands. An eighteenth-century dovecote remains here and can be seen from the road. It was described and illustrated by Donald Smith in his *Pigeon Cotes and Dove Houses of Essex* (1931). Outside the line of a former moat, it is octagonal, of red brick, and with 294 nesting places. Owls and rats led to its demise. This 'Duffus', as old-timers used to call them, may stand where there was another when the seventeenth Earl of Oxford sold the manor.

Second to the church in historic and architectural importance was ancient 'Fremnells', the site now underneath the reservoir. Its destruction is of particular regret, for Pevsner regarded it as the best house of its date in Essex.

In a previous book, *A Discovery of Old Essex*, I gave some account of the house and the manor when writing about the 'mysteries' of Hanningfield Water. In repeating it in substance here, I can now add rather more to the narration of Fremnell's past. The waterworks has an open day in the summer of every year and I can recommend a visit, if only to see the photographs of the house taken before and during its demolition. Throughout the centuries it was owned by several notable families. The name has been traced back to as long ago as 1376 when it was 'Hemanales', taking it from Sir John de Hemenale of the previous century. By the 1500s it was being styled 'Fremanallys'. Later, it was called 'Tremnalls'.

In 1476 it was held by Sir Thomas Tyrell and remained with that family until 1627. With many branches, their greatest single distinction was to claim descent from the Sir

Walter Tyrell whose arrow struck down William Rufus whilst hunting in the New Forest.

In the reign of Elizabeth, Sir Henry Tyrell JP was often at Fremnells, although the family seat was Heron Hall at East Horndon. Fremnells had its own oratory where the Tyrells, staunch though discreet Roman Catholics, could hear Mass in relative safety. In 1627 the manor was sold by Sir John Tyrell of Herongate, and it passed into dual ownership. Then, around 1635, it would seem to have been in the hands of Sir Charles Caesar, Master of the Rolls (1590-1642), for in that year Lady Caesar left a rent-charge of £5 a year out of Fremnells for the relief of the poor in Downham and adjoining parishes.

Its connection with the legal profession continued. Morant gives the next owner as Sir Thomas Raymond, a Justice of the King's Bench. His father was of Bowers Gifford near Basildon. Dying on the Circuit in 1683, Sir Thomas was buried in Downham church. There is a memorial to him here and in the church at Runwell as well. His son Robert became a distinguished lawyer and MP, being raised to the peerage as first Baron Raymond of Abbots Langley in Hertfordshire.

'Soon after' 1683, Morant wrote, the estate was acquired by Benjamin Disbrowe or Desborough. He was the seventh son of the outstanding Cromwellian John Desborough. 'The grim giant Desborough', as Samuel Butler called him, was a yeoman of Cambridgeshire who 'exchanged the spade for the sword'. Trained for the law, he quickly rose to prominence after his marriage to one of Cromwell's four sisters. The list of his offices is a lengthy one. From being the colonel of a regiment of horse, he went on to become a major-general of several western counties; one of the four Commanders of the Fleet in the war with the Dutch; a Lord of the Cinque Ports; and a member of Cromwell's Committee of Safety and the Council of State. He was also given a seat in the House of Lords. These high positions under the Protector brought him an annual state income of £3,236.13s.4d. Among the signs of his gratitude was to name one of his sons Cromwell.

At odds with Parliament and with his own regiment after

the death of Cromwell in 1657, he was compelled to
withdraw to his house 'farthest off London'. Although
Desborough took no part in the trial of Charles I, with the
return of Charles II in 1660, he tried to leave the country
but was apprehended by the Sheriff of Essex near the coast.
He was set free, only to be arrested again and confined to the
Tower on a slender charge of plotting to take the life of the
King and his queen, Catherine of Braganza. He was soon at
liberty, however. Then he went to Holland, where his
intrigues led to his being ordered back on pain of being
declared a traitor. Once more he was imprisoned for a while,
first in Dover Castle and then sent to the Tower for a second
time. Effectively silenced, his last years were spent in
seclusion. He died at Hackney in 1680, aged seventy-two.

Although I have found no documentary evidence that
Desborough was ever at Fremnells, it is most likely he knew
it well. He held land in the county and was a quorum
member of the Commission of the Peace from 1652 to 1659.
This was, perhaps, a nominal and honorary position, for he
attended none of the Quarter Sessions.

One of his sons settled at Bocking. There is little to tell of
his son Benjamin at Fremnells. Despite the stigma on his
name, he must have won civic acceptance after the
Restoration of the monarchy for he became Sheriff of Essex
in 1689. He was thrice married. By his first wife he had a son,
Cromwell. He had no children by his next wife, Sarah, who
died in 1692. She had been married twice previously, both
husbands being merchants of Dutch origin. Benjamin's third
wife gave him five girls. He died five years into the reign of
Queen Anne. The heir, Cromwell Desborough, married his
stepmother's daughter Cornelia, the offspring of her union
with Cornelius van den Anker. Their son, Platt Desborough,
inherited Fremnells. He passed on in 1741, and Morant,
writing some years later, referred to him as the late
possessor.

The family remained in possession of the house until early
last century. It was then, according to Arthur Mee, that
every member in residence there perished in an outbreak of
smallpox.

Fremnells was an Elizabethan house refashioned in the

following century. The Royal Commission on Historical Monuments gave 1670 as the date; '1676' could be seen upon the gateposts. But Pevsner challenged the date and considered the front of the building to be of the 1630s, which would make the alterations pre-Desborough. Much of the house was of timber and plasterwork, and this, along with the chimney-stack of the Hall, was unchanged from the mid-sixteenth century. From that period as well was the linenfold panelling in several rooms.

At an auction not long since I acquired a small guidebook to the county which, from internal evidence, can be placed just prior to 1900. In this *New Holidays in Essex* I came upon the following description of Fremnells. In writing of the mansion's 'air of serene age and security', the editor was not to know that he was giving a later reader its obituary:

> Turning down the Stock Road for half-a-mile, and then a few yards to the right at the cross-roads, one sees a short avenue of poplars. This is the entrance to Tremnales or Tremnels, locally known as the Great Hall, a fair-sized Elizabethan building, now a farmhouse. A low frontage in brick, once red, now pale and mellow with age, broken only by low gables in the centre and extremities; a spacious lawn in front protected by a low wall and a brick gateway surmounted by an arch of iron-work; a moat now confined to the back and sides; such is the outer aspect of the old hall. Within, the rooms are spacious, lofty, panelled in oak from floor to ceiling. Though modern taste has painted the dusky panels in light tints, the change has proved powerless to remove the air of serene age and security which has so long lodged here, an air such as belongs to the cloister or the retirement of a grassy Cambridge quadrangle ....

Today, a house bearing the ancient name and hidden from view by conifers stands some yards to the west of its lost predecessor.

Two final fragments can be rescued from the buried history of this spot. Coller wrote of an old custom of the manor: 'If any person paying quit-rents neglected to do so by twelve o'clock the day they were due, the amounts doubled every hour.' And nearby, at Crows Heath, there once stood a house called 'Disbrowe's Folly'.

4

Winstanley and the Tempest

Littlebury, a mile or so out of Saffron Walden, is a village which has put on substance in our time. On the old highway to Cambridge, now with the M11 running parallel just to the west, it shows a few period houses of note. But its chief attraction is the Church of the Holy Trinity, standing within the outline of a Roman camp. Among the things to draw on here is the carved stone font, and more especially its oaken canopy and cover of Tudor date. Although the church has been much restored, particularly in the chancel, the work has been admired as unusually good Victorian Gothic.

But three centuries ago Littlebury had a more curious rival for attention. Somewhere hereabouts, perhaps a little to the south of the church, stood the residence of Henry Winstanley, engraver, architect and engineer. Insofar as he is remembered at all today, it is as the builder of a lighthouse, a celebrated 'first', yet he was equally a visionary of Fun, a grand master of mechanical entertainments.

Many lie in the churchyard here who must have been of good report among their neighbours. However, you will search in vain for any grave or memorial to 'Eddystone' Winstanley. To tamper slightly with Shakespeare:

> Full fathom five his body lies:
>   Of his bones are coral made;
> Those are pearls that were his eyes:
>   Nothing of him that doth fade
> But doth suffer a sea change
> Into something rich and strange

His father, Henry Winstanley Senior, was a mercer by

Winstanley's house at Littlebury

occupation and a man of local standing. He lived in Saffron Walden. From 1676 until his death in 1680 he was the churchwarden of St Mary the Virgin, and he was also the master of the workhouse in the town. When he was buried in the south chapel of the parish church, he left behind a daughter and three sons, Henry, Robert, and Charles.

Henry's uncle was the William Winstanley of Quendon. He styled himself 'a true lover of ingenuity' and became known as 'the Barber Poet' and 'Poor Robin', a publisher of popular almanacs, verses and other works. He has been credited with *Poor Robin's Perambulations from Saffron Walden to London* of 1698. This has also been attributed to Robert Winstanley, but that William had the *nom de plume* of Poor Robin at the time of his death is evident from an entry in the parish registers of Quendon: 'William Winstanley was buried 22 December 1698 Cognomine poor Robin' (all written in the same hand). It is very likely that either William or Robert hatched and printed the marvellous nonsense of the Henham Serpent. Certainly, both the nephews shared with their uncle a penchant for impish humour.

Of Henry Winstanley's early life and education nothing is known. He married – his wife's maiden name was Taylor – but had no children. He emerges from obscurity first as a 'porter' at Audley End, and then as 'clerk of his majesty's works at Newmarket and Audley End', the king being James II.

The stately house at Audley End, for a short period in royal hands, has been greatly reduced in size from what it was. Its original appearance of palace-like proportions can be seen from the copper engravings issued by Winstanley from his Littlebury house. There are twenty-four in the series: 'Plans, Elevations and Particular Prospects' of the mansion. Without them our knowledge of what the house was once like would be scanty. The plates bear three dedications: to the King, to the third Earl of Suffolk, whose grandfather first built the house, and to Sir Christopher Wren. In that to the Earl, Winstanley wrote that, 'Having seen the most renowned Palaces of France, Germany and Italy, especially from where Architecture was brought over,' he had aimed to bring Audley End House, 'lying obscure and not took notice of', to the attention of the world.

We know what his own house looked like from his engraving of it, clearly a publicity exercise. Ornate, it was two storeys in height, with Dutch gables, a balcony and a central lantern surmounted with a vane. On the front, left of centre, was a clockface. The house is shown fenced, with several obligatory figures placed by a turnstile gate, and it had a walled courtyard or garden at the side. Beyond the latter, at a short distance, there are shown the sails of a windmill. If Winstanley's, it has been surmised as a mill to pump water.

The turnstile entrance led the visitor to a house of tricks. Of these devices there are several contemporary accounts. Celia Fiennes, that most inquisitive traveller, saw the house in May 1697: 'Thence to Little-berry where is a house with abundance of fine Curiositys all performed by Clockwork and suchlike which appears very strange to the beholders but the Master was not at home so I saw no more than the Chaire they set in when they are carried out.' The famous chair was on a rail and took its unwary sitter backwards into the garden, there to suspend him over water. A further report is of another chair, a 'particularly comfortable-looking chair, which, when sat upon, instantly closed its arms around the occupant, making him a firm prisoner'. To this is added: 'A seemingly old slipper when kicked immediately brought from the floor a ghost.' Pepys, on a visit to Sir William Batten's house in 1660, saw a comparable chair: called 'King Harry's, it 'made good sport'.

A German scholar and book-collector, one Zacharia Conrad von Uffenbach, came to England in 1710 looking out for manuscripts and rare editions. While staying at Cambridge he went across country to Winstanley's house. In his *Travels* he noted the chair on rails, a lift to the cellar, and paintings 'most by Winstanley' which left him unimpressed. The picture of Winstanley in the museum at Saffron Walden could be a self-portrait. The displays were continued for some years after Winstanley's death. *The Post Boy* announced in December 1712: 'The fam'd House of the late ingenious Mr Winstanley is open'd and shewn for the Benefit of his Widow with all the Curiosities as formerly: and is lately butifi'd and well furnish'd, and several New Additions made by her ... and is shewn for 12d each and to Livery men 6d ...'

With his keen eye for business, Winstanley took his hydraulic delights to the heart of fashionable London. At the lower end of Piccadilly, by Hyde Park, he established a 'Mathematical Water Theatre' in 1696. Easily located by a windmill on the top, like his house in Essex it continued to be run by his wife after his decease. The entertainment took place each evening 'between 5 and 6 of the clock'. A box could be had for 2s.6d; admission to the pit was 2s, to the First Gallery 1s.6d, and to the Upper Gallery 6d. An advertisement in the original *Guardian* in 1713 gave the treats in store for the special occasion following upon the Treaty of Utrecht: '6 sorts of wine and brandy to drink the Queen's health, all coming out of the barrel, with bisket and spaw [spa] water; and as peace is enlarged there will be added Claret, Pale Ale, Stout, and water playing out of the head of the barrel when it is in the pulley. The house will be particularly adorned this night with several new figures and machines, playing of water and fire mingling with water, and a flying dragon, casting out of his mouth at the same time a large stream of water with fire, and perfumes, and a prospect of the coaches going to Hide Park in cascades of water.'

Ingenious though these extravaganzas were, and novel though they may have been to the crowds, they were not so foreign to that age. The palace gardens and grottos of Renaissance Italy, some of which Winstanley must have seen, had led the way with cunning displays of water, often designed to take the visitor unawares. Yet his genius for such spectacles and pranks doubtless went far to establish their adoption in England. Addison, writing in the *Guardian* (9 July 1713) noted: 'Showers of rain are to be met with in every water-work; and we are informed, that some years ago the virtuossers of France covered a little vault with artificial snow, which they made to fall above an hour together for the entertainment of his present majesty.'

In 1694 Winstanley designed his supreme achievement, the first Eddystone lighthouse, built on the rock seven leagues out from Plymouth. From the print we have, it looks today an almost whimsical construction, more like an Oriental pagoda. Looking at it, with the ultimate tragedy in mind, one is tempted to see it as an essay in black humour.

The lighthouse was completed and ready by 1699. It bore that date, Winstanley's name and various inscriptions on its side, e.g. *'Pax in Bello'*, 'Glory be to God' and *'In Salutum Omnium'*. Made of wood, it had numerous angles and projections, including a windvane and winches, which certainly did not aid its wind-resistance. When its greatest test came, it was on a fearful scale, a disaster to be remembered for a lifetime. On what must have been a very clear day, Celia Fiennes saw it from the battlements at Plymouth in 1698. She wrote: 'On a meer rock in the middle of the sea ... it will be a great advantage for the guide of the ships that pass that way.' To this she added one of her typical moral observations, which was to prove ironic: 'From this you have a good reflection on the great care and provision the wise God makes for all persons and things in his creation, that there should be in some places, where there is any difficulty, rocks even in the midst of the deep which can be made use of for a constant guide and mark for passengers on their voyages.'

Supremely confident, Winstanley had often been heard to voice the desire to be in the lighthouse at the height of a storm, for it had survived not a few. On 26 November 1703 he was on the rock to supervise some repairs. The weather had been rough for several days but that evening a tempest arose. Through the swirl, signals could be seen for help, but come morning the lighthouse and Winstanley were gone. The elements had staged the greatest Water Theatre of them all. Several days later a merchant ship not knowing the news, ran aground on the rock with the loss of most of its crew.

The night of 26 November was fierce all over southern England. Defoe narrated the event in his *Collection of the most memorable Casualties and Disasters which happened in the late Dreadful Tempest, both by sea and land*, published in 1704. He made a special trip to Kent to see the effects of it there. The West Country took the worst impact from the prodigious tide.

Here in Essex, the headmaster of the grammar school at Felsted noted while writing up his accounts: 'Raged so dreadful a tempest, so destructive by land and sea, that History scarce records a greater'. At Purleigh, in the registers, this memorandum was inserted: 'Novem ye 26, 1703 about one of ye clock in ye morning, there arose ye most outrageous tempest that ever was heard or read of in England, it held till seven or eight o'clock in ye morning, it lay'd naked most peoples dwelling houses, Barns, Stables and all other outhouses, and multitudes of them were levelled with the ground, it blew down Steeples, unript our Churches and made thousands of tall and sturdy Oakes, elmes and other trees root and body and branch to submit to ye violence of an outrageous blast, yt brought ym to ye ground and made ym fitt fuel for ye flames.'

Many families suffered bereavement, yet few could have been more saddened than the Everards of 'Langleys' at Great Waltham. The loss of Sir Hugh Everard's second son was commemorated on a stone of grey marble in the parish church. He was only sixteen when taken by the sea, and the inscription records his survival of an earlier storm, with other escapades remarkable for one so young. The last three lines of his memorial must surely be appropriate, as well, to Henry Winstanley in his watery grave:

> This monument
> Covers not the ashes, but perpetuates the memory
>   of Hugh Everard ...
> Not being thirteen years of age, he left Felsted
>   school, September 24, 1700
> And, on the 29th, he went under Captain Whittaker,
>   to convey King William from Holland.
> Though then a tempest arose, which destroyed
>   many in his sight,
> Yet the undaunted youth still had glory in view.
> The invitation of that, and the greatness of his soul,
>   Lessened all the threatenings of danger.
> August 15, 1702, after several voyages and hardships
>   endured
>   by land and sea,
>   A descent being made into Spain,
> His choice and request put his courage upon action.
> Being the third that landed, and the Spanish horse
>   coming upon them,
>   The commander fell by his hand,
> And the sword of the man before grazed the side of
>   the young stripling.
>   But now reader,
> Turn they triumphant songs into mournful dirges,
> For the fateful 27th of November, 1703, comes big
>   with tempest and ruin,
> (Such as former ages never knew, and future will
>   scarce credit),
>   When our brave young man,
> (Having changed his ship in order for new achievements)
>   And crew were swallowed up by the unsatiable
>   Godwin.

Thus fell the age's wonder,
After he had established a reputation
That shall never die.

5

Enigmas of Two Old Houses

Much has come down from our past by word of mouth. Although often garbled and embroidered by fancy or false inference, verbal history should never on that account be despised. The sheer tenacity of village tales calls for respect and explanation. And sometimes the old-time stories yield surprises.

Like every county, Essex has its houses of mystery. Of these there are two I find particularly engrossing: Eastbury House, near the Thames at Barking, and 'Ashlyns', which stood in a remote corner of the countryside. Both have traditions which link them with plots against the throne.

Eastbury House, to be found off Ripple Road, is an Elizabethan, brick-built mansion of moderate size. It bears the date 1572 on a rainwater-head but is likely to be several decades earlier in parts. The date may refer to its ownership or occupation by Clement Sysley, who died in 1578.

Elizabeth Ogborne's *History of Essex* (1814) has a plate showing the house from the rear. The view was drawn before one of its two towers had gone. Both had spiral staircases. The walled courtyard, twisted chimneys and many gables can still be seen today. Beneath the picture is a reproduction of three military figures painted on the wall of a room in the house. Then much obliterated and dating from the reign of James I, they depict a drummer, a fifer and a soldier with a gun and its rest. Ogborne also noted 'sea pieces' in the house. I last went inside as a boy and can recall a cannon and a Roman stone coffin. However, I have no memory of the paintings seen by Pevsner in the Great Chamber, murals of landscapes and seascapes.

Eastbury House, Barking

Coller's impressions of the house were forlorn: 'The mansion has long been partly unoccupied. We found long galleries wreathed with cobwebs and half-filled with lumber – large apartments converted into lofts for hay, corn and harnesses, with remnants of ancient frescoes here and there to be traced on the walls – sad memorials of their faded grandeur; but we rejoiced to hear that this interesting piece of antiquity is likely to be restored.' That was in 1861, and restored it was. Earlier this century it became a museum, and in Arthur Mee's *Essex* (the fifth impression, 1956) there is a good summary of the exhibits. The museum was rather short-lived. Now it is a property of the National Trust and on lease to the Borough of Barking.

The tradition was long persistent that the mansion had figured in the Gunpowder Plot. One version had it that the plan was hatched here by Guy Fawkes and the other conspirators who, had it been successful, would have witnessed the far-off conflagration of Parliament from the top of the tower. A variant tale is that Lord Monteagle was staying here when he received the letter of warning. Both stories have long been totally discounted, but it is intriguing to speculate why the connection with Eastbury House was ever made.

I like to think that I may have hit upon a clue. There was a manor in the district variously given by Morant as Fulkys, Foulkis or Faukes. This was absorbed by the greater manor of 'Jenkins' in Barking, and the house itself had stood in the town. It is tempting to surmise that local people may have pronounced the name as 'Fawkes', which could have led to an identification of the district with the plot, if not initially with Eastbury House itself. The next step would have followed folklore 'logic', making the link with the most impressive house of the period left in the neighbourhood. Its very setting would aid the imagination, with the look-out towers giving a panoramic view of the river and the capital in the distance.

As for the Monteagle connection, his seat was at Great Hallingbury, but an article on the Thames dykes in the *Essex Review*, written in 1903, affirmed that, 'In the reign of James I, Eastbury was tenanted by the first Lord Monteagle, son of Lord Morley.' However, I know of no evidence ever produced for the contention. (Monteagle did have a house to the west in Bethnal Green.) The writer added: 'Now only a small portion of the house is habitable, sufficient for a tenant farmer, while bats and owls claim the bulk of the building.' Such was its condition forty years after Coller had made his observations.

Eastbury House, despite its tribulations, is now well cared for. This has not been the fate of ancient 'Ashlyns'. Long lost from sight, there is not even a description of it.

I first learned of Ashlyns one bleak and rainy day, the kind that makes me turn either to the bookshelves or to music. I was browsing through *Kelly's Directory of Essex* for 1933 when I came upon an entry under High Ongar which much intrigued me;: 'ASHLYNS, otherwise Gapps, 3 miles north-west, a hamlet in this parish, is remarkable for an ancient mansion here, now a farmhouse: here Thomas Howard, 4th Duke of Norfolk, KG, is said to have concealed himself when charged with high treason for abetting Mary Queen of Scots; he was eventually beheaded 2 June, 1572, and buried in the Tower.'

Now this struck just the right note demanded by the hour. My curiosity was aroused, for I had never heard of such a hamlet or house before, nor, indeed, of the episode. So I reached for my copy of William White's *History and Gazeteer of Essex* of 1848 for some confirmation. Here I read, again for the parish of High Ongar: '... Astelyns, otherwise Gapps, belongs to the College of Physicians in London, by gift of Dr Harvey, in 1672. The ancient mansion in this manor was surrounded by a moat, and had a park of 100 acres. In this house the unfortunate Duke of Norfolk was for some time concealed, when charged with high treason, for acceding to the proposal of marrying Mary Queen of Scots.' Looking up Coller, I found the story repeated. He, too, attributes the gift of the house in 1672 to a Dr Harvey, not to be confused with the celebrated William Harvey who died in 1657.

I spent the next few hours piling books high upon my desk, but there were only two other references to be found. Under the Howards in Addison's *Essex Worthies*, he has this: 'While visiting Audley End, Elizabeth discovered incriminating evidence, and the duke was arrested in hiding at Ashlyns, near Ongar', which is affirmative if bare. Morant also records the tradition that Norfolk 'is said to have concealed himself there'. He gives the information that, 'The lands lie partly in Bobbingworth, and North Weald. It has now no Court or Quit-rents. There formerly belonged to it a

seat, moated round; but is now a mean farmhouse, or cottage
... Dr Baldwin Harvey of the College of Physicians
purchased it, and settled it, in 1672, on that College, who are
present possessors. The Estate contains three hundred thirty
seven acres.'

With no older sources cited, I knew that there was a long
and delightfully problematic trail ahead of me.

The first puzzle which immediately arose was the very
location of Ashlyns, for looking on the map three miles
north-west of High Ongar village takes one well outside the
parish boundaries. Reaney's *Place-Names of Essex* gave rise
to further initial complications. He lists four Ashlyns, two of
them with variant spellings. There is Ashlyns just inside
Shelly; Ashlings in Magdalen Laver near the boundary with
North Weald (this one was 'Astelyns' in a sixteenth-century
rental); and the manor of Ashlyns given for High Ongar.
Each derives its name from the family of a Richard Ascelyn
here in the fourteenth century, and they are manorially
related. There is also an Ashlings Farm in the south of High
Ongar, which, because of its position, cannot be the one in
question. Morant's remarks were to give me the lead.

There is no Ashlyns to be found within the boundaries of
High Ongar today, yet a map of the Essex hundreds and
parishes as they were in Elizabethan times shows 'detached
portions' of the parish, and their location accounts for three
of the Ashlyns given above. No longer within extra-
parochial land, the Ashlyns cum Gapps I was looking for lies
to the west of Bobbingworth Lodge, and south of Weald
Lodge and Bowlers Green. On Chapman's map of 1777 it is
marked 'Great Ashleys', and on the present Ordnance
Survey map it is shown with a moat to the rear.

So much for tracing its whereabouts. One small mystery
was solved, but as for the story of the fugitive peer, it must
remain unverified by firmly documented fact. Whatever its
status, it does speak of an Essex link with the Howards
which certainly holds a few miles to the north in the county.

The Essex historian Holman, writing in 1735, described a
fine stained glass shield to be seen in Finchingfield church. It
depicted the armorial bearings of the Howard family. This
has long been no more, gone without trace along with other

treasures of the church from medieval times. It is thought the shield was probably the gift of Agnes, Duchess of Norfolk, after being widowed in the 1530s. A few years later, in 1541, the third Duke of Norfolk became the lay rector of Finchingfield as a result of Henry VIII's seizure of the monastic properties.

The rise and fall of the fourth Duke was spectacular. Said to be second in wealth only to Queen Elizabeth, he married three times. By his first wife, the Lady Mary FitzAlan, he had his eldest son, Philip, Earl of Surrey and later of Arundel. Mary died in childbirth, aged only seventeen. Norfolk's second marriage was to Margaret, the daughter and heiress of Baron Audley of Audley End, Saffron Walden. She gave him five children, and it was from one of her girls that the Sackvilles of Knole were descended. She, too, died young, in 1564, in her early twenties. The third Duchess was similarly ill-fated, dying in 1567, just a year after being wed.

Thomas Howard now became disastrously involved in the Ridolfi plot, designed to free the imprisoned Mary, Queen of Scots. What happened, with all the allegations and Norfolk's eventual trial, can be found summarized by Sir William Addison in his book on Audley End.

Philip was fifteen when his father was executed. After marrying Anne Dacre, he became a fervent Roman Catholic. But he was not to escape the royal suspicion and wrath. Eventually, in fear for his life and with Anne expecting his second child, he made plans to leave the country and for his wife to join him later. But he was apprehended, placed in the Tower and brought before the Star Chamber to be fined a crippling £10,000. He was confined at Her Majesty's pleasure for the remaining ten years of his life. Camden has it that he died as the result of his religious austerities.

After a period of harassment, Anne went to live and bear her child in the old parsonage at Finchingfield. Not only was it a family property but the living had been leased to the friendly Robert Kempe of Spains Hall. Moreover, she had co-religionists in the neighbourhood, particularly at Braddocks or Broadoaks, Wimbish, where the Wisemans had constructed priest-holes.

So it was that Anne, Countess of Arundel and Surrey,

gave birth to the next Thomas Howard at Finchingfield on 7 July 1585, as he noted in his will at the end of his prestigious life. Shortly after her delivery, Anne went to London and so far as we know never went back.

The role of Ashlyns stays obscure. Morant's narrative on the small estate mentions a Thomas Ayliffe of 1517, after which the records seem silent for the next 150 years. Even the date of its demise as a manor and the demolition of the house remains unknown. Yet if the Duke came here, it must surely be that he took his brief refuge with a household sympathetic to him. It would help if the name of the owner or tenant at that time could be discovered. Certainly, the isolated location of the house, deep in the countryside in a maze of lanes, would have commended itself as a retreat from prying eyes. It is still problematic to find it today, as I was to learn when I ventured there.

A good map or a local informant is essential. The route I chose to follow was through Moreton, two miles out of Ongar. The village is one of my favourites in mid-Essex. In 1985 it had the honour of being judged the Best Kept Village in the county. To get from here to Ashlyns you take the road to the Lavers, bearing left all the time. Bushes, a lovely house, is on the way, and Ashlings in the spacious parish of Magdalen Laver. (The latter, standing beyond a moat by the wayside, is a superb late-medieval or early-Tudor dwelling. Its front, the best view, has a continuous jetty, but this can be seen only from the drive.) Moving on, one turns left at Weald Lodge, where a signpost to the Green Man may draw you off course. A few moments along from the Lodge, a narrow, winding road marked Ashlyns Lane branches to the left. When you have passed a house or two (one called Kings Pieces), which constitutes Bowlers Green, Ashlyns itself comes into view on the left.

Of no great age, the farmhouse stands up tall and white and with three conspicuous dormer windows. With the kind permission of the owner, Mr Collins of High Laver Hall, I have been able to trace the line of what is left of the moat. (I was led to it by a very alert and informative youngster.) The moat, two sides surviving at right angles, lies to the very rear. Being late summer, its banks were densely overgrown and invisible until we were right upon it. Much has fallen in, and debris has aided the disfigurement down the years. But from what I could see, it was once of considerable width and extent, one side trailing off to become a very lengthy ditch. It is clear the old house must have been of a fair size, occupying what is now a spacious farmyard. However, it would need an expert to calculate its original dimensions, so much having gone.

Although there is little of antiquarian interest for the traveller to see here, there is as always in the heart of Essex the appeal of the land. It is a spot, as well, at which to pause and reflect upon this long-lost fragment of a vanished England. On these lanes you should have no difficulty in peopling the past with the third eye of your imagination.

6

Fame and Seclusion at 'Otes'

Just a mile or so to the north of 'Ashlyns', you will discover, after some searching perhaps, the site of another once-notable house which has fallen to iconoclastic Time. This was 'Otes' in High Laver, although a later dwelling in the vicinity has proudly annexed the name. High Laver is one of the three Lavers, farming parishes, which despite the nearness of built-up Harlow to the west keep a quietness and isolated feeling in the rural heartlands.

There is more than one type of landscape in Essex, and the very diversity is for many the great attraction. Only in one or two places can we say it approaches grandeur. None come here for sublimity. Instead, once we escape the towns and housing estates, we find a highly domesticated countryside; intimate, full of green-ringed pockets. The scenery in the main is muted, giving contentment rather than magic, and lending itself to unhurried contemplation. To the temperament and cast of mind of the philosopher John Locke, it gave an ideal setting.

Setting aside students of philosophy and of the history of political ideas, there cannot be many to whom John Locke is more than a name, if that. Nor can his association with a pastoral retreat in Essex be widely known. He was the only philosopher of stature who came to live in the county, choosing to spend his long retirement at Otes with a family which later was to enjoy royal favour, only to see their potent influence at Court dramatically eclipsed.

John Locke was born in Somerset in 1632. He received his early education at home, in a Puritan household but one free from the sharper extremities of the breed. In the family circle, his tuition in old-time virtue, discipline and

'Otes' at High Laver in the time of John Locke

knowledge was so rewarding that he was ever the advocate of private schooling. He then went to Westminster School, which he did not relish. The formidable Dr Busby ruled there then, and Aubrey said of him, he 'hath made a number of good scholars, but I have heard several of his scholars affirm that he hath marred by his severity more than he hath made'. Locke, however, was not averse to recommending the rod to correct the young delinquent.

From Westminster he went on to Christchurch, Oxford, where, after graduating, he was to spend thirty years. He showed himself no friend of fanaticism. Theology was among his studies, and he read the works of Descartes and the newly published *Leviathan* of Hobbes. He became a member of the Royal Society, at first founded at Oxford as a Philosophical Club before it transferred to London, and he briefly practised medicine. His life was very active despite the poor health which always dogged him.

Locke formed an enduring, if unlikely, friendship with Lord Ashley who became the first Earl of Shaftesbury. Keenly interested in politics, Locke was appointed by Ashley to be his confidential secretary.

It was at Exeter House in the Strand that he began his consuming inquiry into the nature of how man acquires his knowledge, an analysis of sense-perception and the manner in which our ideas arise from it. What he thought at first could be encapsulated on a single sheet of paper was to result many years after in his famous *Essay Concerning Human Understanding*, produced, he said, in 'incoherent parcels'.

With the downfall of Shaftesbury Locke began his first period of exile, going to Montpellier and Paris. Returning in 1679, he kept a most discreet silence when his former employer was again under a cloud. After trial and imprisonment in the Tower, the Earl was released and went to Holland, where he ignominiously died.

Long before this, Locke must have been acutely aware of the character and motives of his patron. Never can two associates have been so unalike, and Locke surely felt a strain upon his loyalty. The career of Antony Ashley Cooper, Lord Shaftesbury, was one of cynical opportunism and infamy, adept at changing sides from the Civil War onwards. He created the first of our political parties, the

Country Party, later to be nicknamed the Whigs. His life-long ambition was to castrate the monarchy. A thoroughgoing sceptic, his was the controlling intelligence behind the notorious Popish Plot, orchestrating the nation-wide hysteria.

Locke, having been closely watched and spied on during these events, once more went abroad. His return to Oxford was expressly forbidden. Six years later, following the accession of William of Orange, he came back to England.

Now at the height of his powers, Locke had begun his *Letters on Toleration* and his two *Treatises on Civil Government*, as well as publishing his great *Essay*. He was radically opposed to 'enthusiasm', an expression which then signified the flush of religious excitement and personal revelation. In all his diverse philosophy, calm light has pre-eminence over heat, sense over sensibility. Not a vast system-maker, no builder of an intellectual cathedral, as a philosopher he is best labelled with that definition given by Plato: 'a lover of wisdom'. Bertrand Russell also gave him an accolade, styling him 'the apostle of the Revolution of 1688' and adding: 'the most moderate and most successful of all revolutions'. With Newton and with Hume, he ranks, too, as a precursor of the French Enlightenment.

Such was the man who around 1690 first went to Otes as a visitor. Then, through inclination and advancing age and seeking relief from his asthma, made tortuous by the 'London smoke', he decided on complete rural seclusion. He went to his friends the Mashams at High Laver, just over twenty miles from the centre of London, where the capital, in John Clare's words, was 'nothing but a guess among the trees'. And here he lived, an honoured and much-loved guest, for his remaining fourteen years.

At this point I must interrupt my narrative on John Locke to fill in some of the earlier history of the Masham family and their country home, a house which already had social distinction.

The manor was possessed by a John Otes in the reign of Edward II. The Suliard family (who figure in Chapter 2) held part of the estate from late in the fifteenth century until shortly before 1610. Then it came into the hands of Sir William Masham, whose ancestors had originated in the north of England but eventually settled in Suffolk. Very soon, Sir William acquired the rest of the manor, and Otes stayed in the family until the death of the last Lord Masham, the second baron, in 1776. He had no children, so the title became extinct.

Sir William was a baronet and related to the Cromwells of Hinchingbrooke. As might be expected, he rallied to the side of Parliament against the Crown. In 1638 Oliver Cromwell was at Otes, in particular to see Mrs Oliver St John, his first cousin, who was staying there. Carlyle in his *Letters and Speeches* was to note: 'Mrs St John came down to breakfast every morning in that summer visit of the year 1638, and Sir William said grave grace, and they spake polite devout things to one another; and they are vanished ... all silent, like the echoes of the old nightingales that sang in season, like the blossoms of the old roses.'

Sir William prospered. He was three times MP for Maldon, and then for Colchester. He was a minor voice in the land, serving on Cromwell's Council of Thirty-Two after the execution of the King. Another William, a grandson, followed as the second baronet. He died unmarried, so the title passed to his brother, Sir Francis Masham. His second wife was Damaris, and this is where we can resume with the life of Locke.

The house to which he came, after, in Lady Masham's words, 'having made trial of the air of this place', was a Tudor building. A rare old print shows it square, substantial and in parts with battlements. The front was gabled. There was a lawn and an ornamental lake fringed with lime trees. Otes was demolished close on 200 years ago, but the lake, much diminished, and a moat can still be traced.

Locke was given an apartment, a bedroom and a study, but lived in with the family. For his board and lodging he paid £1 a week. He had a manservant, and his quarters must have been spacious for I have read that he had a library here of 4,000 books. At first, he was still publicly active, making journeys to London to fulfil his duties as Commissioner at the Board of Trade. He would return exhausted, but such were the healing properties of Otes and its green shade that within hours he was restored in body and spirit. It was not long before he rarely left his new small world.

However, this does not mean he lived in total isolation. There was the daily companionship of the family, particularly Damaris. Lady Masham clearly treasured his presence. A charming and deeply meditative woman, one of her tastes was for metaphysics, Locke's *bête noir*, but this does not seem to have disturbed his regard for her. He spent much time meditating on the Bible, while she produced two devotional works. He wrote here *Some Thoughts on Education* and his essay *The Reasonableness of Christianity*, a treatise more ethical than doctrinal. As his days grew shorter, he was preoccupied in reconciling intellect and faith, belief accommodated by reason. His well-tempered approach to religion was a far cry from his solid Puritan upbringing. It was to become a hallmark of eighteenth-century Protestant thought and conduct, decorous and un-extravagant.

Compared with the fullness of his life before, it could be said of Locke at Otes what Sir Henry Wooton remarked on his fishing – 'An idle time, not idly spent'. He wrote to a friend in Ireland, striking a note of reassurance: 'I wish you were here with me, to see how well I am, for you would find that, sitting by the fireside I could bear my part in discoursing, laughing and being merry with you, as well as ever I could in my life.' He loved to ride through the lanes and, ever glad of congenial company, conversed with the rector, Samuel Lowe, on matters spiritual and local. Lowe died five years after Locke, having ministered to his parish for forty-seven years.

Great men came here as well from the wider world to see the ageing philosopher, among them Sir Isaac Newton to discuss theology, and almost certainly another academic friend, Sir Robert Boyle, whose sister, the pious and gifted Mary Rich, had died a few years before at nearby 'Leez'. We can be sure that Locke never in this house had the experience of Dr Johnson who, on an occasion of dining at a friend's, came away to say indignantly, 'Sir, we had *talk* enough, but no *conversation*; there was nothing *discussed*.'

This reminds me of that story in the *Spectator* of Locke's being invited to dine with three lords, one of them Shaftesbury. After the meal, 'instead of conversation, the cards were called for, where the bad or good Success produced the usual Passions of Gaming.' Locke retired to a window and began to write. One of the noblemen asked him what he was putting down. 'Why, my Lords,' Locke answered, 'I could not sleep last Night for the Pleasure and Improvement I expected from the Conversation of the greatest Men of the age.' Steele added: 'This so sensibly stung them, that they gladly compounded to throw their Cards in the Fire if he would his Paper, and so a Conversation ensued fit for such Persons.'

The end came serenely for John Locke as the autumn leaves fell in 1704. Just prior to his departure, he took the Sacrament, and Lady Masham read to him from the Psalms. To quote his generous will, he died 'in perfect charity with all men and in communion with the whole Church of Christ, by whatever names Christ's followers call themselves', a most fitting farewell from this great advocate of toleration.

The inscription on his memorial in the parish church of All Saints, the words in Latin composed by himself, commands attention with its opening lines:

Stop, Traveller,
Near this place lieth John Locke.

The tablet used to be outside but is now within on the south wall of the nave. Translated, the epitaph continues:

If you ask what manner of man he was,
he answers that he lived content
with his own fortune.
Bred a scholar, he made his learning
subservient only to the cause of Truth.
This thou wilt learn from his writings
which will show thee everything else
concerning him
with greater truth than the suspicious phrases
of an epitaph.
His virtues indeed, if he had any,
were too little for me to propose,
as matter of praise to himself
or as an example to thee.
Let his vices be buried together.

As an example of manners, if you seek that,
you have it in the Gospel.

....

This stone
which will in a short time perish
records
that he was born
August 29, 1632,
that he died October 28, 1704

There is one final episode to be touched upon in the history of the Mashams. Four years after the burial of Locke, Lady Masham died and was buried at Bath. Her husband lived on till 1724. Samuel, his son, in turn inherited. With him, and through his scheming wife, Abigail, the family was lifted briefly to a dizzy and precarious height of national importance.

Abigail Hill, as she was before her marriage, was the daughter of a merchant trading with Turkey, one of his twenty-two children. It was through the good offices of her aunt Sarah Churchill, Duchess of Marlborough, that Abigail was introduced to Court and became a lady-in-waiting to Queen Anne. It was a filial gesture which the Duchess, with her moral dominance over the Queen, was to live to regret, to put it mildly. Soon Abigail was well and truly 'in' and had the ear of her royal mistress. She married Mr Samuel Masham and engineered the rise of her brother to the rank of general. The great friendship between Anne and the Duchess cooled, to end in mutual bitterness with Sarah Churchill being excluded from the Queen's household.

Abigail Masham's influence behind the political scene was remarkable, although the lack of precise detail enables us to see what happened only in silhouette. The manoeuvring for place and power about the throne on the eve of the Hanoverian succession is a complex affair. The picture is not helped by the somewhat enigmatic figure of Queen Anne herself, a sovereign who has never clearly 'emerged', unlike so many others. She vacillated in her support of Whigs and Tories (it was a time of coalitions) and for the greatest man of the hour, John Churchill.

Abigail, related as well to the moderate Robert Harley,

exerted herself in support of the ultra-Jacobites in the Tory ranks, working for the succession of the Stuart 'Old Pretender' as James III. It was a palace revolution they sought to effect, seemingly with the acquiescence of Anne. All was going well. One of our most notable historians, G.M. Trevelyan, has commented that they needed five months, perhaps at a pinch five weeks, to mature their plans. But capricious Fate took a hand. The Queen had long been afflicted with dropsy. Suddenly she worsened, and her death in five days aborted the design. 'Fortune,' wrote Swift, 'turned rotten at the very moment it grew ripe.' Quickly, the bewildered, feudal-minded George of Hanover was acclaimed, arriving later from Germany for his coronation with a vast entourage. 'Not a mouse stirred against him, in England, in Ireland, or in Scotland.'

Just as swiftly, Mrs Masham left the scene, withdrawing in total obscurity to Otes, where she was to remain fretfully for twenty years until her death, virtually incommunicado and in exile, watching from afar her coterie go one by one to their graves. The sole records of those hidden years are apparently only moss-grown tombstones near the chancel: Abigail, 1734; her brother, 1735; her husband, 1758; and finally her sister Alice, 1762. Alice was seventy-seven. She, too, had found room at the top, having been a lady-of-the bedchamber of Queen Anne.

Can there be another unsophisticated place where two such diverse careers were enacted to such differing ends? Standing by the church or by the vestiges of Otes, we could be tempted to share a passing mood of Walpole's: 'I don't know how it is, but the *wonderful* seems worn out.' He meant the disappearance of the novel and the curious. I have often felt that. But in putting our ear to the ground for these voices from the past, it is more rewarding to say, as Isaac Walton said in another context, that they are 'worthy of a room in the memory of a growing scholar'.

7

The Fanshawe Connection: 'In Cruce Victoria'

In the opening lines of his account of the old hundred of Becontree, with its nine parishes, Philip Morant wrote in the 1760s: 'It abounds with Villas, where the rich and industrious citizens retire, at this convenient distance from the thick Air and Hurry of London.' This description does not, of course, apply today, two centuries later, and would be somewhat more suitable now for Surrey. The eastern suburbs of the City, with their rural aspect and seats of the gentry, have long since been swamped by what Dickens called 'London over the Border'.

Among 'the rich and industrious citizens' were the Fanshawes, who had properties in Barking and Dagenham and at one point in time held the paramount lordship of the entire hundred of Becontree. The line reached the height of its distinction prior to the Civil War. Without exception, its members pledged themselves to the Crown, giving their services and fortunes to the cause. They never recovered their full style at the Restoration, and thereafter the name of Fanshawe slowly descended below the horizon like a fading star.

The family had its origins in Derbyshire. Thomas Fanshawe, on coming south for London to take up the post of a clerk in the Exchequer Office, bought the Barking manor of 'Jenkins' in the year 1557. He rose quickly, for in 1561 he became Remembrancer of the Exchequer, an office of the Crown responsible for collecting the debts owed to the sovereign. He was one of three members of the family to hold the appointment in succession. It was Thomas who established the wealth and status of his descendants. Through his two wives he founded the Hertfordshire and Essex branches of the family, namely at Ware Park, the main seat, and in Barking and Dagenham. Prior to his death in 1600 he gave Jenkins to his son, Sir Thomas Fanshawe, whose death occurred in 1631. Another son, William, bought the Dagenham estate of 'Parsloes' in 1619.

Jenkins has vanished from sight and from the map, unlike Parsloes, which has at least survived as a place-name. The earlier history of Jenkins is of no small interest because of its connections.

Upon the closure of Barking Abbey in 1539 and the seizure of its lands by Henry VIII, the capital manor of Barking stayed in royal hands until James I sold it to Sir Thomas Fanshawe for £2,000, although reserving a rental of £160 per annum. Linked with it was the smaller manor of Jenkins. However, with the end of the nunnery, this had gone into private hands. Among its distinguished owners prior to the Fanshawes was Edward Osborne, ancestor of the dukes of Leeds.

Although not mentioned by Morant, the Osbornes also held Parsloes for a brief period. They probably had it after Sir Rowland Heywood, Lord Mayor in 1570, whose name appears in Morant's account of the manor. The will of Hewet Osborne of Parsloes is extant. Dated March 1599 and proved the following year, it shows him to have been a Turkey merchant and much concerned for his wealth on the high seas. Such sea-lane anxieties were common among his profession, as Shakespeare expressed it in *The Merchant of Venice*, where he has Salario say to Antonio: 'Your mind is tossing on the ocean .... Believe me, Sir, had I such ventures forth, The better part of my affections would be with my hopes abroad.' Among Hewet Osborne's many bequests, he left four houses in London, 'late the inheritance of Edward Osborne, knight deceased'.

To return to the Fanshawes, Morant tells us that the widow of Sir Thomas, namely Lady Anne, née Bebington, 'who was a Lunatic', held Jenkins for the King from 1632. Her son, Thomas, born in 1607, took on the house. He was

'Parsloes', Dagenham, in 1905

made a Knight of the Bath at the coronation of King Charles
I. But in the family tree, it is Sir Henry Fanshawe who is of
greater importance than those at Barking and Dagenham, for
he was the father of the eminent Sir Richard.

Sir Henry resided at Ware in a fine house which has gone.
Many years after his death in 1616, his granddaughter,
Anne, wrote of his garden at Ware Park that there was 'none
excelling it in flowers, physic herbs, and fruit, in which
things he did greatly delight'. She added: 'Also he was a
great lover of music, and kept many gentlemen that were
perfectly well qualified both in that and the Italian tongue.'
He was noted, too, as a fine horseman.

He died at the early age of forty-eight and lies in the
family vault in the parish church at Ware. He left five sons
and five daughters. One of his sons, Sir Simon, was 'a
gallant gentleman, but more a libertine than any of his
family'. The eldest boy, Thomas, fought for the King at
Edghill, which led to the ruination of his estate. A few days
before the coronation of Charles II, in April 1661, he was
made a Knight of the Garter at Windsor, the first time this
ceremony had been held for twenty years. That same year
Sir Thomas became the first of the five viscounts in the
family, the last dying in 1716. But despite these honours he
was not reimbursed for his losses. He died in 1665.

His brother, Sir Richard Fanshawe, was also a staunch
supporter of the monarchy during the years of the Rebellion.
A classical scholar of repute, a poet and translator, after the
death of Cromwell he was with Charles in exile. He was on
familiar enough terms with the royal family for them to call
him 'Dick'. From the outset of the Civil War his life was full
of escapades and travels. With the defeat of the Prince at
Worcester, in 1651, Richard was taken prisoner and brought
to Whitehall but, through the entreaties of his wife, released
on bail. Joining the Prince in exile, he was knighted in the
Netherlands, at Breda. He was promised by Charles the
office of Secretary of State, but on the return of the King to
England he was passed over, in Sir Richard's words, for one
'that never saw the king's face', a shameful act attributed to
the jealousy of Lord Clarendon. In his last few years he
continued in the diplomatic service. He was sent on an

embassy to Lisbon and then made Ambassador to Madrid. And it was there, awaiting recall, that he died of an ague in 1666.

His widow, Lady Anne, distraught and with her children 'all young and unprovided for', brought back his embalmed body to Tower Wharf and to a London devastated by the Fire. Sir Richard was placed at first in All Hallows, Hertford, but was later transferred to Ware.

Financially, Anne was shabbily treated. Among the arrows which pierced her heart was the sale of Ware Park for £26,000 to a London brewer. 'Thus,' she wrote, 'in the fourth generation, the chief of our family [Thomas, the second Viscount] since they came into the south, for their sufferings for the Crown, sold the flower of their estates, and near 2000 a year more. There remains but the Remembrancer's place of the Exchequer office: and very pathetical is the motto of our arms for us – The victory is in the Cross.' She parted with much of her own property, including her lease on Fanton Hall, presumably Great Fanton Hall, a house which was of Jacobean origin in North Benfleet.

It would take far too long here to do justice to the *Memoirs* of Lady Anne, which she wrote for her 'most dear and only' surviving son, four years before her demise in 1680, at the age of fifty-five. First printed in 1830, my copy, a collector's piece with the added rarity of photographic illustrations, is that published by the Bodley Head in 1905.

The *Memoirs* are a work of no small charm. They convey without impediment the very air and spirit of the times, a romance in the best sense of that word. Although the Lady Anne, like Madam Eglantyne, 'was all heart', her courage burns time and again upon the page. With fluency she carries her reader along with her tale of love and tribulations. Her days were crowded with events: at home, at Court, on land and sea, in England and in foreign parts, in settings of luxury and privation, amid a cavalcade of names and faces – with several compelling narratives of the supernatural – imparting all to her boy from an inner view, all the more personal and authentic for being private. Her story ends abruptly, a fractured sentence in a broken life. Our knowledge of the Fanshawes in their prime would be thin and colourless without it.

Lady Anne's son died in 1694. He was but thirty-four, and a fever, it is said, had rendered him deaf and dumb. The Viscountcy came to an end in 1716 with the death of the fifth Viscount.

The *Memoirs* have little to say of Jenkins or Parsloes, where minor branches endured after the eclipse of the main lines of the family. The Fanshawes of Jenkins ceased in 1705, there being no male descendants, and the house went around 1718, the estate having been bought by the antiquarian Smart Lethieullier for £40,000. Portraits and other heirlooms, many from old Ware Park, went to Parsloes and to William Fanshawe of Great Singleton in Lancashire (from whom were descended the Fanshawes of Dengie in Essex). Jenkins, with its timbered house lying within a moat, was a mile from Parsloes.

Of Parsloes, rather more can be told. By 1900, then still in the family's hands, it was in a very bad way, as can be seen from a photograph of that time, showing the walls shrouded in vegetation. In 1848 White had described it as 'a large brick mansion with an embattled pediment and turrets, in a small park about a mile west of the village, and is the seat and property of the Rev T.L. Fanshawe. It was new fronted in 1816.' The alterations gave it an appearance of Strawberry Hill Gothic. It had some panelled rooms and several carved stone fireplaces acquired from Eastbury House, never a Fanshawe property.

The Rev. Fanshawe was the vicar of Dagenham for forty-one years. His eldest son, John Gaspard Fanshawe, the ninth of the family in succession to own Parsloes, died just after Christmas in 1903. His obituary in the *Essex Review* tells us that in a long life he had been private secretary to a number of statesmen and public men, and was a member of several learned societies.

After just over 300 years, the family finally gave up Parsloes in the First World War. By 1905 the fine library had been dispersed and the grounds were being used by the Essex Trotting Club. The house was demolished by the LCC when it developed the huge Becontree Council Estate.

In 1927 H.C. Fanshawe published a history of the family, and in more recent years Captain Aubrey Fanshawe RN presented a series of old family portraits to the Borough of Dagenham. They are displayed in Valence House, fine canvasses by distinguished masters. Here Lady Anne among many others blindly meets our curious gaze. Locked in their past, they look out from their frames, motionless, calm and assured in a world not ours.

8

Past and Present at Gosfield Hall

When I first ventured to Gosfield Hall, I went with no high expectations. On a classic day in June, I had lunched with my sister at the Bell in Castle Hedingham, that jewel of a village, and afterwards climbed the lane to the magnificent, cool Norman keep. Then, as we headed the short distance south with these delights behind us, I anticipated something of an anticlimax. From photographs, I envisaged a building with but partial merits, marred, I feared, by ill-assorted styles. I knew it had long been shorn of its grand estate, and deprived of the artistic treasures and furnishings which had reached their apogee with the residence of Samuel Courtauld. I knew in advance, as well, that many of the apartments, over eighty rooms in all, were not open for inspection. But to see the long gallery where the first Elizabeth had walked was the principal object of my visit, and the celebrated lake. Above all, the long line of eminent men who had lived in the house, and made its fame, had aroused my greatest curiosity.

So it was with muted hopes that I left my car parked in the shade on the drive. What I was to see turned out to be one of the most rewarding surprises in the Essex landscape.

Gosfield Hall stays little known to the public at large and does not rank as a major tourist attraction. Formerly a stately home, it was saved from extinction by the preservation orders of Essex County Council and through being acquired from them by the Wayfarers Trust after the last war. It is now owned by the Country Houses Association. As a lovely

The west front of Gosfield Hall

retreat for around thirty elderly people of means, it has not gone all-out to publicize itself. It would, in fact, be hard-pressed to cope with a substantial, daily flow of visitors. No bold notice at the entrance, or in the village on the A1017, tells that it is open two afternoons of the week throughout the summer, when it can be viewed by a conducted tour. All here is seclusion, privacy and peace, ten minutes drive from crowded, energetic Braintree. For the lover of tranquillity with style, of period architecture, the resonance of the past, and sheer greenery, the Hall with its five acres of ground and surrounding farmland will be no disappointment. It is *par excellence* a place 'where (in the words of Shakespeare's *Henry V*) nothing so becomes a man as modest stillness and humility', even though most of its distinguished occupants were far from self-effacing.

The west wing of the mansion is the oldest part, early Tudor, and stands on even earlier foundations, presumably the home of Thomas Rolf, a Sergeant-at-Law, who died in 1440. The red-brick Hall, built by Sir John Wentworth around 1545, was quadrangular in plan, and the courtyard remains, restored in the sixteenth-century style and very attractive. It has a fountain in the centre which, on the day I was there, splashed refreshingly in the shadows.

The rooms of Wentworth's house around this courtyard were just twelve feet in width. Of these, the gallery on the first floor, 106 feet long, is outstanding. Known as the Queen's Gallery, for it was used and admired by Elizabeth when she came here on a royal progress twice in her reign, it is superbly panelled on both sides along its full extent. It is now the dining-room, each resident contributing his or her own table upon arrival. An engaging feature in the gallery is the two small windows, so angled as to serve as spyholes down on the entrance to the house and yard. Originally, for defensive purposes, there were no outer windows on the ground floor. The two there now are nineteenth-century additions.

Seen from the outside, the west front is picturesque. The warm brickwork of the façade, diapered in places, is set off by the sombre green of ancient yews. Above the four-square gateway arch, the ground paved here with wooden tiles, but not the originals, there is a six-light window, a gable above that with a clock, and then an elegant cupola. Chimney-stacks with polygonal shafts grace the skyline. The projecting bays at either end of the front were added last century but they aid the pleasing symmetry.

On the death of his father, Roger, in 1539, Sir John Wentworth inherited the Gosfield estate along with numerous other manors in the district and in Suffolk. Little seems to be known about his public career or of the man himself, apart from his having served in Cardinal Wolsey's retinue. When he died, aged seventy-three in 1567, he was succeeded by his only daughter, Lady Anne Maltravers. Thrice married, she was by then a widow and childless. Upon her decease and burial in the parish church, St Katherine's, in 1580, the property went to another Wentworth, the son of her uncle. He died in the year of the Armada and was followed by his son, another Sir John, who 'being extravagant, wasted his estate'.

The will of Sir John Wentworth who was the Hall's creator gives us an insight into his wealth and his household. He left a vast quantity of plate, which he bequeathed in part to his wife and daughter, and to his nephew Henry Wentworth. Among the many valuable articles he specified were numerous 'hangings', i.e. tapestries, one depicting the story of Moses, carpets, cushions, two of cloth of gold, and a variety of bedding. His armour went to his nephew John. From the will, we also learn the names of some of the rooms: the Chief Chamber, Lord Wentworth's Chamber, the Parlour and the Old Parlour with its Inner Chamber.

After the Wentworths, the next owner to leave a conspicuous mark on the house was Sir Thomas Millington. He bought it in 1691 off a Mr Grey and carried out the first major alterations. He has been credited with changing the east wing, building the Grand Salon or banqueting hall, and in doing so created the so-called Secret Chamber. This is one of a number of rooms at the Hall to have beguiling names.

On the corridor outside the butler's pantry, you will be shown a row of antique bells and, below each one, boldly marked on a label, the name of the room from which came many an urgent summons. Among others there is the King's

Room and the Queen's Room (once occupied by Louis XVIII
of France and his wife), the Wentworth Room, the Nugent
Room, the Priest's Room, the Painted Chamber, the Blue
Room, and the Prophet's Room. The last of these refers to
William Juniper, the 'Seer of Gosfield', and you can read of
him in the next chapter. The Queen's Room, I am told, is of
particularly fine workmanship, so much so that its occupant
may not do any interior decoration. This has to be left to
experts.

Sir Thomas Millington was an MA and MD of Oxford
University, President of the Royal College of Physicians, and
a founder member of the Royal Society. He was First
Physician to William and Mary, and to Queen Anne, which
was how he received his knighthood. He died in 1704 and
was interred in the Wentworth Chapel of St Katherine's. He
was much in demand among the gentry. He is mentioned in
the *Autobiography* of Sir John Bramston the Younger, who
sent for him several times to alleviate his complaints and
those of members of his family at Screens in Roxwell.

Millington's Grand Salon, flooded with light from tall
windows, is impressive in its proportions: forty feet long,
twenty-nine wide and thirty high. It is into this room that
the visitor first steps today. The ceiling is painted, the central
oval with allegorical figures the work of Sir James Thornhill,
the remainder in *grisaille* with corner medallions
representing Titian, Raphael, Michelangelo and Correggio.
The old portraits to be seen here now have no connection
with the history of the house, but they relieve what would
otherwise be very stark and intimidating walls. In the days
of the Courtaulds, portraits of five generations of their
family looked down. Then, massive oak chairs carved with
their coat of arms stood here, and *The Fruit Gatherers* of
Murillo hung over the fireplace. The Italian chimney-piece of
marble remains. But pride of place was given to a full-sized
copy of that Hellenistic masterpiece, the Laocoön. Reputed
to have been acquired by Napoleon in Italy, it was packed
for transporting to Paris but never despatched because of
Waterloo.

An ornate Jacobean chest, large and yet like all else in this
room dwarfed by the setting, is worth a close look. This was

presented by Sir Adrian Boult, whose father was a close friend of Samuel Courtauld. Elsewhere in the house, framed pieces of excellent needlework by Sir Adrian's mother can be seen, and a photograph of his father, showing a most striking resemblance to the great orchestral conductor.

In constructing the banqueting room, the ceiling was taken up to $1\frac{1}{2}$ storeys, and this resulted in the Secret Chamber above it, little more than a tall man's height and covering the same area as the great hall; access is by a trapdoor from above, and then by a step-ladder. There are signs it was once in use. Not so today, and dark and without windows it is not, of course, part of the itinerary. In its silence, the walls must guard a lost tale or two, but not, it seems, as a hiding-place. Every word from below can be clearly heard here.

Millington's son John inherited upon his father's decease, but his tenure did not last so many years. A sheriff of the county, he died in 1714. Having no children, he willed the estate to his two sisters, but within a year they had sold to John Knight, Esquire. Four times returned to Parliament, he was a Justice of the Peace and a Lord Lieutenant of Essex.

Knight made yet further changes to the house. A new, severe north wing was constructed; that it was under his direction seems established by his crest figuring on its old drainpipes. Some of the Tudor gables were left but concealed from view. The original windows facing the courtyard also stayed, but the two upper rows are windows in appearance only, being blind and bricked in behind. The principal room, which takes up most of the first floor, is a fine ballroom, dominated and enhanced by floor-to-ceiling mirrors at either end. These, I was told, were installed by Louis XVIII during his residence – it is said he was always intensely conscious of what was going on behind him. Once, an impressive pair of chandeliers hung in this room but they now adorn a merchant bank in the City.

John Knight barely passed middle age, dying at fifty in 1733. Previous to his decease, he left his properties to his wife Anne. He had been her second husband, and with his exit she married Robert Nugent, years later to become Earl Nugent and Viscount Clare. He was a character indeed and like so many characters probably better read about than encountered in the flesh.

Nugent was Irish, born in 1702. It has been said of him that in addition to being handsome, he was 'endowed with a vigorous constitution, an athletic frame, a stentorious voice and a wonderful flow of spirits'. He also had a flair for marrying rich widows who secured him 'places, pensions and peerages'. He was notorious, too, for his amours, even in that licentious age. When Nugent married Anne Knight, 'an ugly and obese dame', she ordered the marble tomb which she had erected for her late husband in the parish church to be screened off, although she hardly ever attended worship there. Nugent's marriage brought him the parish of Gosfield, a seat in Parliament and around £100,000. The union was to prove childless and without lasting happiness. They argued, then separated. Anne died in 1756.

Nugent was fortunate in his connections. He was a close friend of Oliver Goldsmith, who was no stranger to the Hall, but more important for the future Earl was his friendship with the Prince of Wales, lending him large sums of money, never paid back, but Nugent was recompensed with titles when the Prince became George III. He was twice MP for Bristol and owned the borough of St Mawr in Cornwall.

His pursuit of wealthy ladies and his liaisons gave rise to a drawing room expression: 'to Nugentise'. In calling him 'old Nugent', Horace Walpole explained to a correspondent: 'It is not merely to distinguish him from his son; but he is such a champion and such a lover, that it is impossible not to laugh at him as if he was a Methuselah.' His indiscretions were numerous. One of his affairs was with the young Lady Essex. At a crowded supper party, when he was discussing with her some proposed alterations to her house, his wife 'in the softest infantine voice called out, My Lady Essex, don't let him do anything out of doors but you will find him delightful within!'

Horace Walpole went to Gosfield in July 1748, where he remained several days and was taken to see Castle Hedingham. He gave his impressions in a letter to his friend George Montague, written from Mistley where he had been staying with another connoisseur of architecture, Richard

Rigby. 'Hemingham Castle,' as he styled it, 'where Harry the Seventh was so sumptuously banqueted, and imposed that villainous fine for his entertainment, is now shrunk to one vast curious tower, that stands on a spacious mount raised on a high hill with a large fosse. It commands a fine prospect, and belongs to Mr Ashurst, a rich citizen, who has built a trumpery new house close to it.' But Walpole was far less gracious about Gosfield Hall:

> I suppose you have heard much of Gosfield, Nugent's seat. It is extremely in fashion, but did not answer to me, though there are fine things about it, but being situated in a country that is quite blocked up with hills upon hills, and even too much wood, it has not an inch of prospect. The park is to be sixteen hundred acres, and is bounded with a wood five miles round; and the lake, which is very beautiful, is of seventy acres, directly in a line with the house, at the bottom of a fine lawn, and broke with very pretty groves, that fall down a slope into it. The house is vast, built round a very old court that has never been fine; the old windows and gateway left, and the old gallery, which is a bad narrow room, and hung with all the late portraits, but so ill done, that they look like caricatures done to expose them, since they have so much disgraced the virtues they pretended to. The rest of the house is all modernised, but in patches, and in the bad taste that came between the charming venerable Gothic and pure architecture. There is a great deal of good furniture, but no one room very fine: no tolerable pictures. Her drawing room is very pretty, and furnished with white damask, china, japan, loads of easy chairs, bad pictures, and some pretty enamels.

Such were Walpole's mixed feelings about the Hall. His critique may not have been ours, but it comes from an arbiter of excellence whose vision of antiquarian style and elegance was highly individual and taking on substance in his own house at Strawberry Hill.

But there was one thing in the house which did command Walpole's admiration without reserve, and to this there is an intriguing history.

The architect Sanderson Miller (chiefly remembered now for his work at Hagley Hall) wrote to Lord Dacre in 1768

giving the details of how Mrs Nugent came to put up a
'Curious Chimney Piece' in the library at Gosfield. About the
year 1736 he went with her to Halstead and while in the
vicinity found a house which 'looked like the Remains of an
old Seat'. This was, in fact, Bois Hall, which has quite gone,
leaving a Bois Field which marks the site of the estate. It was in
this house that Sanderson Miller first saw the chimney-piece.
Its attraction was a white, alabaster mantel, which, carved in
bold relief, portrayed the Battle of Bosworth Field. The figure
of Richard III lay beneath his charger, surrounded by twenty-
four helmeted combatants on horseback, many of whom
could be identified by the arms on their shields. At either end
of the crowded tableau stood miniature figures of Henry VII
and his queen.

Learning that the house belonged to Lord Tilney, Miller
told Mrs Nugent of his find. She wrote to his lordship,
offering him another marble chimney-piece in exchange
'which would please the Farmer's wife much better'. Tilney
agreed, and on having it taken to Gosfield she had it cleaned
and the gilding restored. Miller thought it must have originated at Hedingham Castle, and this is almost certainly
correct. It bore the shield of John de Vere, thirteenth Earl of
Oxford, whose seat was at Hedingham. He was at the battle,
where he was in command of the main force of Lancastrian
archers.

This relic of the past remained at Gosfield Hall until the first
Duke of Buckingham and Chandos acquired the house early
last century. He had it removed to his magnificent seat at
Stowe. When this house in time became a public school, it
remained *in situ*, saved by subscription.

Until early this century there was another rarity at Gosfield,
and extremely curious. For many years a life-size wax effigy
of Lady Nugent stood in the parish church and later in the
long gallery of the Hall. Dressed in black silk and with a poke
bonnet, her likeness was seated in a glass case. She was
represented sewing and had a bloodstained bandage on a
finger. Local folklore had it that this signified the manner of
her death, punished for plying her needle on the Sabbath.
What is certain is that the effigy was a relic of bygone ritual in
which such figures were carried in funeral processions.

After her death Robert Nugent married Elizabeth, daughter of the Earl of Berkeley. This, too, became an ill-fated match, for they separated and he disowned the second of their two girls. In 1766 he became a peer, as Viscount Clare and Baron Nugent, and for the next year was President of the Board of Trade. In 1776 he was created Earl Nugent. He died twelve years later, at the age of eighty-six. His third wife outlived him. He left one legitimate son, Lieutenant-Colonel the Hon. Edmund Nugent. He was painted by Gainsborough (the Earl had sat for him twice). Edmund Nugent seems to have vied with his father in boudoir intrigues, having several natural sons, one a Field Marshal and C-in-C in India, while another was an Admiral.

In the diary of Joseph and John Savill, clothmakers at Bocking, an entry for 8 November 1788 reads: 'Lord Nugent was brot from Dublin, where he died, through Bocking to be interred at Gosfield. Lay in state one night at the Queens Head Inn here.'

How much he contributed to structural changes at the Hall is debatable, but the superb landscaping was largely his and worthy, as Arthur Young observed, of 'Capability' Brown. The imposing lake, one mile in length, was his creation, although Millington is thought to have begun the project by joining up two small brooks. No longer part of the Hall's property, the lake is the largest expanse of inland water in Essex. Now often used for water ski-ing, it is up to Olympic requirements for the sport.

The reconstructed south front of the house was for long attributed to Nugent but is now regarded as more likely to be earlier than his occupation. Plain and white and very elegant, it has seventeen bays. On the ground floor in the centre is the library, a somewhat sombre room with dark, ornate woodwork, and a ceiling papered to imitate marble. Another nice deception is a door lined with the spines of old volumes to pass as a bookcase.

The south range faces the lawn, flanked by two sculptured stags, and gives a distant glimpse of the lake. One of the attractions for me in walking around the outside of the Hall is the sensation of looking at four different houses and moving through several centuries in a matter of yards. There are stately trees, too, to draw the eye, among them Californian Redwoods, and at the north-east corner of the building a truly mighty cedar which sways and creaks ominously when the wind gets up. Standing to the north on another lawn backed by shrubbery there are several statues, two of them Venus and Adonis, I was told; yet I think from their appearance they are the figures mentioned in Courtauld's day as 'The Maiden preparing for a Bath' and 'The Tired Huntsman', both by Bailey. On this side of the house there is another rare and unexpected survival. Here are two well-houses, one covering the great well itself and its pumping station, unfortunately beyond restoration, with the other containing the wheel once worked by a horse. The yoke is still in position.

With the passing of Nugent, his elder daughter married George Greville, the first Marquis of Buckingham, who took into his name that of Nugent-Temple. His acquisition of the old Earl's estate brought him its income of £14,000 a year. The Marquis and his wife won local renown as benefactors. A school was established, meals were provided for the poor, and they introduced the straw-plaiting industry to the area. This did not catch on until they appeared in the village and in church wearing be-ribboned straw hats.

In 1807 the exiled Louis XVIII of France and his consort were offered the house as a refuge by the Marquis. (They had declined a government offer of Holyrood House.) The Savills noted in their diary that November: 'Compt De Lille came over from Russia to Gosfield Hall when he assumed the title of king of France with his nobles about him, was visited by most of the French Noblesse in the kingdom.' With an entourage of several hundred, and their own chef, they stayed the best part of two years. They were joined by the King's nephew, the Duke of Angoulême, and by his duchess. This peaceful foreign invasion endured long in the memory of the village, not least the entertainment enjoyed by the locals of being allowed into the Grand Salon to watch the uncrowned monarch and his courtiers dine, a custom which in England had gone with the Stuarts. As a memorial of his presence, Louis left his mark upon the landscape by planting a number of elms. The principal chamber he occupied no longer has his four-poster bed and grandiose wardrobe.

The second Marquis became Duke of Buckingham and Chandos in 1822. He had been christened Richard Plantagenet Nugent Bridge Temple, with a crest to go with each name! He seems to have given little to Gosfield and certainly took much, stripping the Hall of the furnishings which linked it with the past and having them removed to Stowe. It was there and at their other palatial homes that the Buckinghams became fabled for their largesse.

The Hall was now leased to a succession of tenants, the last of whom was E.G. Barnard, MP for Greenwich. He went bankrupt. Then in 1854 the house was purchased by Samuel Courtauld, and with him the residence enjoyed a new lease of life and a final flowering.

Courtauld's distinguished and enterprising family was of Huguenot descent. The Essex branch won pre-eminence with Samuel, who provided work for so many in the north of the county and who laid the foundations for Courtauld's as an international giant. He saved Gosfield Hall from dereliction and transformed the interior. The extent to which this was achieved can be gauged from Coller's account of his visit. He was very enthusiastic. 'Even as we approach the village,' he wrote, 'we cannot but mark the change which the great magician, waving the all-powerful wand of money, has wrought in the domain.'

The house was lavishly adorned with *objets d'art*. Courtauld installed his own gas supply, not only for utility but for effect, so that even a fine pair of alabaster vases would glow in the dark. He also had gas lamps erected along the drive. A great benefactor in the district, he built a large school, a clubhouse and reading-room, and model houses in the village for his workers. Several are still there today. He once said to a friend with some humour, 'When I die, I should like to have written on my tomb, He built good cottages.' He stands out as one for whom industry and the arts were in alliance.

His philanthropy and love of fine things were hallmarks of later members of the family. The next Samuel Courtauld (1876-1947) founded the famous Institute of Art in 1931. He gave thousands to the Tate Gallery, of which he became a trustee, and for long was chairman of the National Gallery's Board of Trustees. His daughter married R.A. Butler, who was to become Lord Butler of Saffron Walden. She died in 1954, and later 'Rab' Butler married the widow of Augustine Courtauld, noted for his Arctic exploration. It was through the connection with the Butlers that the portraits in the Grand Salon came to the Hall.

When Samuel Courtauld Senior died in 1881, at the age of eighty-eight, the house with its park, then of 300 acres, went to his adopted daughter, Mrs Lowe. (He left his other daughter £90,000.) Mrs Lowe lived at the Hall until shortly before the last war. It was then used by the military and afterwards as a home for evacuee children. After this it stood abandoned and was saved from demolition at the eleventh hour by the intervention of the Council.

Such then is the partial chronicle of an historic old house. No one family has resided here for any great length of time. Most, however, have given it visible distinction. And if so much has gone which marked their passage, there is the colour of their lives to enhance the picture.

The future of Gosfield Hall should prove far less eventful. One evening shortly after my first excursion to the house I took down the *Essays of Elia* from the bookshelves. The old, worn volume fell open at the last lines of 'The Superannuated Man'. As I read them, I was sure that those who have chosen to see out their days at Gosfield would identify at once with Brother Lamb in his retirement, set free from his desk at the India House:

> I am Retired Leisure. I am to be met with in trim gardens. I am already come to be known by my vacant face and careless gesture, perambulating at no fixed pace, nor with any settled purpose. I walk about; not to or from. They tell me, a certain *cum dignitate* air, that has been buried so long with my other good parts, has begun to shoot forth in my person. I grow into gentility perceptibly. When I take up a newspaper, it is to read the state of the opera. *Opus operatum est.* I have done all that I came into this world to do. I have worked task-work, and have the rest of the day to myself.

9

Characters and Worthies of the Church

Not for the first time I have been reading Sir William Addison's *The English Country Parson*, a book with great warmth for its subject, and I have yet again been struck by the range of personalities among the old-time clergy. One sentence from his opening chapter aids my own small theme.

Addison is in a village somewhere in England and sets an archetypal scene. He narrates a conversation with an elderly cleric in his vicarage garden, a quiet, reflective man and 'something of a botanist'. The parson remarks: 'We are a mixed lot, of course. The Church has had its full share – perhaps more than its share – of humbugs; but I have always believed that the best of us have kept alive something of great value.'

That 'something' is impossible to define neatly. Perhaps it is a sense of perennial roots, of continuity, and decencies which struggle to survive. It is rarely made tangible, yet is real enough. Among the poets, who are our diviners, Betjeman is one of those who convey the aura most. But much of the 'something' must lie in the lives of those who left their mark upon their congregations, and sometimes on the wider landscape of the Church they served.

There is no typical parson, despite the stereotypes of screen and stage. I must stress this, for the few Essex figures I am selecting here represent only part of the great variety to be found in a very differentiated class, a class set apart by vocation and not always by birth and breeding. They are diverse in talent, idiosyncrasies, temperament, religious

St Andrew's, Sandon

persuasion and worldly interests. They are, indeed, a 'mixed lot' in claiming to stand beneath one banner.

Each of the men I present to you is a stranger to this age of 'improved means to an unimproved end'. Their passion is curious because it is not ours. Material comforts and the quality of physical living are our preoccupations. These are the newer obsessions, hedonistic and decidedly non-

Christian. If you find these characters uniquely odd in being so totally committed to the primacy of the soul, it is because they heeded that devastating rebuke in the Book of Revelations: 'Because thou art lukewarm, and neither cold nor hot, I will spew thee out of my mouth.'

There have been lone visionaries and prophets who courted signs and wonders. One who earned ridicule as well, even among those who shared his doctrines, was William Sedgwick of Farnham. A contemporary called him 'a pious man with a disordered head'. He held the living for ten years from 1634. Then he left to become 'the apostle of the Isle of Ely', where he had been invited as a lecturer, then the term for a guest preacher brought in from outside to deliver a special sermon. In an age of wordy disputation, he gained a reputation for particular ardour, and moved in and out of several Puritan sects. As a mouthpiece of the Lord, he claimed personal revelations and was conspicuous for his warnings of a heavenly wrath to come. Once, 'seeing' the Judgement at hand, he visited some gentry at a house in Cambridgeshire and, finding them neglectfully playing at bowls, admonished them and proclaimed that the End was due within a week. This earned him the title of 'Domesday' Sedgwick, as did his practice of foretelling in the pulpit.

He published numerous tracts. The oddity of several of their titles reflects not his eccentricity but the fashion current in evangelical literature at that time, e.g. his eleven sermons collectively called *Some Flashes of Lightning in the Son of Man*. To read the titles of such works I find an amusing pastime in itself.

Some of my favourites for quaintness can be found in David's *Annals*. Jeffrey Watts of Great Leighs came out with this fine piece of invective in 1657: *A Scribe, Pharisee, Hypocrite, and his letter answered; Separates Churched, Dippers Sprinkled, or a Vindication of the Church and Universities of England*. In the closing years of Elizabeth's reign Stephen Gosson was the rector at Great Wigborough. He had written the *Schoole of Abuse, a pleasant invective against Poets, Pipers, Players, Jesters and Such like Caterpillars of a Commonwealth*. It was dedicated to Sir Philip Sidney, who replied with his renowned *Apologie for*

Poetry. Then there is Firmin's *Establishing Against Shaking; or, a Discovery of the Prince of Darkness, scarcely transformed into an Angel of Light, powerfully now working in the deluded people called Quakers.* Whole pages could be filled with them. There can be few such long-winded counterparts in more modern times, although I was pleased to come across this by a nineteenth-century American author, Eleanor H. Abbott – *Being Little in Cambridge When Everybody Else Was Big!*

Sedgwick took one of his books to Charles I in Carisbrooke Castle, *The Leaves of the Tree of Life,* as though the King had not suffered enough. He managed it in part, and then handed it back with the words, 'I believe the author stands in need of some sleep.' Sedgwick does not appear to have been put out by the slight but 'departed with seeming satisfaction'.

Like so many other dissenters, he was ejected at the Restoration. For a while in London, he died in obscurity shortly after 1668.

A book that Charles would have savoured was the *Eikon Basilike* (the Image or Portraiture of the King). When it was first printed, immediately after his execution, it was attributed to Charles the Martyr himself, describing his ordeals in 1649. There are some grounds for thinking that a pre-publication copy was sent to him on the Isle of Wight. It rapidly went through forty-seven editions, doing much to redeem the faults of the King with a population already feeling revulsion at his judicial murder.

It is now generally accepted that the writer was John Gauden, the Dean of Bocking. When he became the Bishop of Exeter, he laid claim to the authorship. Although he had conformed under Cromwell, he had continued to write in defence of the Church. Born in the remote Dengie village of Mayland, where his father was the vicar, he was educated at Bury St Edmunds, Cambridge and Wadham College, Oxford. He became the Dean of Bocking through Archbishop Laud. He enjoyed great favour on the return of Charles II, getting Exeter and then Worcester, but not the richer see of Winchester to which he aspired. While Gauden was in Essex, he must have heard of 'Domesday' Sedgwick, even if he did not meet him. But he was to know at first hand a far more engaging prophet.

During his short term at Exeter as its bishop, Gauden published a small volume called *The Strange and Wonderfull Visions and Predictions of William Juniper, of Gosfield in Essex, Relating to the Troubles of England*, printed in London in 1662 and sold 'at the Star in St Paul's Churchyard'; there is a copy in the British Museum Library.

He had known of Juniper for some years. Not a cleric, but very much a religious character, the man was employed as a bricklayer by Squire Wentworth. The squire, Gauden wrote, 'sometime told me merrily that Goodman Juniper had strange Fancies, Dreams and Visions, but withall that he was a very honest man'. At first the Dean took little notice of the local soothsayer, 'supposing him to be but a weak and crazy-minded man, whose simplicity and honesty were the best apology for all he said'. But in the spring of 1649 Juniper, having one night been 'commanded', went early to the deanery where Gauden was still in bed. Admitted to his chamber, Juniper starkly told him he had a message from above that the Dean should preach 'Holinesse to the Lord'. Repeating this solemnly three times, he then withdrew and hastened through a wet morning to sound 'the same Alarme' to other ministers in the neighbourhood.

After this startling visitation, Gauden continued to hear of the man from Wentworth and 'the strange confidences' he had 'of a Revolution and Restoration of the Church and Kingdom'. Public report and Gauden's curiosity were such that eventually he sent for Juniper. He answered the summons on a 'faire Summers morning'. The men walked and conversed in the privacy of the deanery garden. William Juniper, 'now above Sixty years old', faced a searching but sympathetic inquisition. 'I seriously conjured him as in God's sight to tell me the truth of things.'

The layman, apparently showing no sign of being intimidated by the occasion, began by telling the mode of his revelations: 'Sir, the experiments I have had of these impressions at sundry times upon my mind in the night have been both sleeping and waking, or as it were between both; I suppose they begin in my sleep, and when I am assuredly awake they do still continue with so quick and clear representations to me, that I cannot well distinguish the difference of them as to my imagination, either sleeping or waking. They are always so exactly the same in my mind and memory, they make so deep impressions on me, that I never forget them. All particulars are still the same before me, as they first appeared.'

Their genesis as narrated will at once be familiar to any reader versed in the testimony of premonitionary and religious experience. They are characteristic as well of hypnogogic phenomena, those seemingly objective, 'out there' images which can accompany the onset or departure of sleep.

Gauden asked him, 'What was the first instance in this kind which made him take notice of such Fancies beyond Ordinary Dreams.' Juniper had been married seven years, and his wife had remained childless. Having 'besought God with more than ordinary earnestness of devotion', he dreamed he had a son, and saw him wearing 'a party-coloured garment'. His prayers were answered and his dream confirmed, for his wife 'unwittingly made its first Coat of a stuff so coloured that I saw in my Dream'. This inaugurated a series of dreams of a highly symbolic character, akin in nature to the like of Pharaoh's, representative of traumatic national events yet to materialize. This is how Juniper de-coded the bizarre details of his own. But the instances he gave to John Gauden (too lengthy to be treated here) are more to be attributed to his intense religious and political hopes and anxieties than to anything really indicative of the paranormal.

The Dean was impressed, if not fully convinced. He was certainly struck by the man's character. 'He assured me that he did not delight to tell these things as having any boast in them; nor did he usually doe it, but sparingly to some sober friends, as occasion offer'd, and they desired.' The inspired bricklayer was no Sedgwick.

The garden meeting was the one and only face-to-face encounter of substance. A year or so later Juniper was dead. The worthy Dean gave this judgement on him: 'Of a very sober and settled mind, so very constant, exact, and conscientious in what he said or did, that he was a plain man, of no great fancy, reach or invention, of no vapour, flash or ostentation, but pious, honest and prudent.' That is no mean epitaph for a humble yet remarkable village workman, rescued from oblivion by the pen of a bishop.

Gauden ends his account by 'offering these things to sober and wise men, who can better judge of proportions between the Predictions and their accomplishments'. His attitude to a possible pre-cognitive element in dreams is that of a Christian humanist, un-dogmatic, open, and cautious. He added: 'A presaging power may sometimes, through little crannies and crevices, look forward and foresee things to come beyond its senses .... Dreams are as pebbles on the sea shore, of various formes and colours, none like another. Yet among them sometimes splendid and precious stones, no way to be undervalued or lightly cast away.'

While Gauden was at Bocking, an even more eminent churchman was the rector of Sandon. Brian Walton, who hailed from Yorkshire, was granted the living in 1635. He had been at St Martin Orgar in Martins Lane, where, it was claimed, 'He was a man of unquiet and unpeaceable carriage.' This complaint almost certainly came from a caucus among his parishioners, opposed to any taint of ritual and defence of the episcopal system. Walton was noted for not mincing his words and, quite unlike Gauden, was not averse to confronting the Puritans head on. St Martin Orgar was, in Stowe's words, 'a small thing'. Virtually destroyed in the Fire, a later tower remains.

When he was admitted to Sandon, he also received the incumbency of another London church at the same time, that of St Giles in the Fields. Like many of the clergy then, he was a pluralist. He was to hold two further offices: that of a prebendary of St Paul's, and chaplain to the king. The St Giles which Walton occupied was the new one of 1623. Its costly furnishings were despoiled by the Puritans, and the parish was where the Great Plague of 1665 first broke out.

Walton's first wife died in 1641, the year before he was deprived of his livings by the Presbyterian party. Her epitaph on marble, composed by himself, can be seen at Sandon in St Andrew's. When the second blow fell, and having ignored with contempt a summons from Parliament, he eluded a move to apprehend him and went to the relative safety of Oxford. This was a stronghold of Charles I, and many an ejected Royalist parson took refuge there.

It was at Oxford that Walton made for himself a reputation for erudition which long endured. With assistance, he worked on and all but completed there his *magnum opus*, the Polyglot Bible, printed in six folios in 1657. It was in seven languages and cost £8,000 to publish. The Plume Library in Maldon possesses an edition. He seems to have been left undisturbed in his academic labours. The first issue had a restrained dedication to Cromwell. Later it was replaced by an extravagant one to Charles II.

When the wind of change blew again, Dr Walton was reinstated. He was back at Sandon for a few months in 1660, but in the December of that year he was consecrated Bishop of Chester. The honour came too late for his enjoyment. Barely a year after, he died in London and was buried in Old St Paul's.

I can find little of Walton the man, apart from his preferments and his learning. Many visit the church at Sandon, noted particularly for its splendid brick tower with a peculiar little dome, and thought to be the work of Cardinal Wolsey's builder at Hampton Court. Yet few in the parish today know of its once distinguished rector, which is why I have considered it fitting to make a small memorial of him here.

Ralph Josselin at Earls Colne would have been quite lost to sight were it not for two pieces of good fortune. He left no weighty books to mark him out for posterity, but he did keep a diary, and it has survived. Its pages not only are of first-rate importance to the social historian, with their individual viewpoint on parochial life and the ripples of wider events in the troubled decades of Josselin's century, but also give us an exceptional insight into the mind of a Puritan minister. He speaks to us as no textbook can, with a living pulse and no eye on publication.

Josselin was born in Roxwell in 1617. Books, especially books on history, sacred and profane, absorbed him in his boyhood. His father recognized his aptitude and sent him as a petitioner to Jesus College, Cambridge, where he took a BA and an MA. Ordained by the Bishop of Peterborough, he must have caused a stir, for he would not follow the other candidates in the 'idolatry' of bowing towards the altar. His parents' home was at Steeple Bumpstead where he often returned 'for want of means', and it was there that young Ralph was deeply influenced by the minister. After much searching for a congenial appointment, he became a curate in Buckinghamshire. He then moved to Cranham, by Upminster, where he ran the school. But his stay was short. A year later, in 1641, and now married, he was invited to Earls Colne. So his arrival there all but coincided with Walton's sequestration at Sandon. Josselin remained at Earls Colne until his death forty-two years later, resisting several lucrative offers to go elsewhere. In June 1674 he wrote in the diary: 'Wore a new gown and cassock, my old one still being in use after 35 years of age; an old friend and a new heart are good.'

He was a moderate in his dissent. Although no firebrand, he was a typical Puritan in his attitude to ritual, images, popular sports and pastimes and, of course, Sabbath observance. One entry in his diary reads: 'This day I heard and then saw the youth openly playing the catt [a ball game] on the green; I went up, rowted them; their fathers sleeping in the chimney corner.' He was opposed to the age-old customs of Christmas, 'jollity and vanity', but he was not against hunting. 'This day in the fields I found a buck; Mr R.H. was with me with his greyhounds; after much sport we killed her in the river; this was an unexpected providence.'

Most of the time his parishioners responded well to his counselling and admonitions, although not all could keep to the straight and narrow. He was regarded as a good preacher. His emphasis, it would seem, was on the good life of piety and its rewards, and not on the punishments awaiting the sinner. He certainly passed the test for sheer stamina and endurance, once giving a sermon which took five hours to deliver, while another lasted most of a day! Several were printed, a common practice, and one was read before the Lord Mayor of London. (A quotation on p. 110 will indicate their flavour.)

Josselin was the first of the clergy in Essex to take the oath of loyalty to the Commonwealth. He was well informed for his time on national and international affairs, and gathered much 'intelligence' on his travels as an army chaplain in the Civil War. When hostilities approached his village, the Royalists marching through to Colchester, his house was ransacked. He took refuge for some weeks with his close friends the Honywoods at Marks Hall. But like Mary Rich and others who shared his beliefs, he was very disturbed at the execution of Charles. 'I was much troubled with the blacke providence of putting the king to death; my tears were not restrained.' He seems to have lived with that as a hideous *fait accompli*. When the Restoration came, he took it in his stride but lived on a knife-edge of anxiety. He was formally suspended, but to his continual surprise no action was taken to deprive him of his living.

He was very concerned about the 'Great Noise of people called Quakers ... sad are the fits at Coxall [Coggeshall] like the pow wowing amoung the Indies'. Alias the Shakers, they were then noted for convulsions or trembling, brought on, according to their doctrine, by visitations of the Spirit. Josselin noted the forty-day fast of a prominent local member of the sect which ended in his death. 'Its said in the contry that his partie went to Colchester to see his resurrection again.' The man had been buried in the castle yard.

Ralph Josselin kept up his devotion to reading, often done at the fireside or by candlelight. Most of the books in his library were of a pastoral or theological character, but they included the works of the Jewish historian Josephus, and *Hygiasticon: or the Right course of preserving life and health unto extreame old age*. He was much concerned with his health. In his last years he wrote: 'If man's age bee 70, then I now being in my 58 am almost at my Friday midnight, lord fitt me for a blessed sabbath at hand.'

He noted down his dreams, which makes a particularly interesting feature of the diary, and there are several veiled references to what could be sexual impulses, e.g. 'My mind very full of roving thoughts in my wife's absence.' There are instances, too, of a fascination with apocalyptic matters. He

was given to reflecting on the timing of the Second Coming.
One summer month he saw a 'remarkable cross' in the sky,
and later two armies fighting in the air. However, I doubt if
his level of credulity in portents is much at variance with
what can be found at large today. He believed in the
possibility of witchcraft, as did most others then, being one
facet of the current world-view which saw a cosmic
hierarchy with agencies of good and evil. But the one or two
cases brought to his notice aroused in him more curiosity
than suspicion.

The diary abounds in entries on his income and how it
was deployed. He farmed, much of his land being leased out,
and kept a record of his taxes. There are notes on the harvest
and on the weather with its vagaries. The total dependence
of life on agriculture is copiously evident. His observations
on the freak Christmas of 1674 reveal he had an eye for
nature: 'Warme, dry, calme Christmas, grasse springing,
herbes budding, birds singing, plowes going, a little rain only
in two days.' The next few days were frostless, 'though some
dayes cleare sun shining, moon and starrs appearing by
night: most persons said never such a Christmas known in
the memory of men; yet I suppose 37 years before the like
and one said 46 or 47 was such an one'.

His mode of thought was also often allegorical. He could
seize upon a little incident to moralize upon his life. An entry
for September 1644 demonstrates this well. It also contains
an example of homoeopathic folk-medicine. 'Stung I was with
a bee on my nose, I presently plucked out ye sting, and layd
on honey, so that my face swelled not; this divine
providence reaches to the lowest things. Lett not sin oh Lord
that dreadful sting be able to poyson me.'

Josselin was not a man at peace with himself. His diary
indicates again and again that he was beset with worries,
physical, financial, but above all spiritual. A Calvinist,
questions of sin and salvation loomed large in his thoughts.
His was not what William James styled 'the religion of
healthy-mindedness' but was one of radical pessimism, so
thorough as to be perverse to those who sail through life
with a sunny disposition. Perhaps Josselin's greatest
anguish was to have to carry his cross beneath his own roof.

His married life was commonplace in its ups and downs but grew more problematic as time went by, or so he hints. He had ten children, four of them sons. He grieved at the deaths of two of his boys, both called Ralph, one ten days old, the other thirteen months, and at the death of Mary, aged eight. John, his only surviving son, was a source of acute and continuous disappointment, pursuing 'an ill course of life'. Ralph Josselin blamed him for debauchery, swearing, drunkenness and the like. His prayers for his son's reformation were of no avail, and he was clearly stunned when he heard that John had secretly married.

Josselin's diary cannot rank in appeal with more celebrated journals. Setting aside the greater landmarks in the genre – Pepys, Evelyn, Parson Woodforde, Kilvert – it does not match the scope, the minute social observation and the passing show of Crozier's, the Maldon miller, or the Great War diary of the Reverend Andrew Clarke at Great Leighs. With these we are in a very different mental climate. They look out through more windows. Josselin's is also lacking in the all-engaging element of *joie de vivre*. There is much, too, it leaves unanswered about the whole man. A diary is rarely if ever to be taken as the full portrait of the writer, and it would be unwarranted simply to assume that Josselin in his pages is typical of all others in his position who held the same creed. But having said these things, the diary stands unique for its time, a rare glimpse of a world which has passed away, and pre-eminently of an individual in that alien land. No mere chronicle of events, it is confessional, and in its psychology shows acute concerns parallel with our own, of which civil disorder and the end of the world through nuclear disaster cap all the rest.

The blood-letting which marked national life when Josselin was alive was virtually over by the time of the Glorious Revolution in 1688. Fanaticism had run its course, and the emotions let loose were exhausted. There followed an era of growing political stability. Matters of religion were more restrained, eventually to become quite sedate and even stagnant, with a philosophic calm prevailing in the apologetics of belief. These were the years which produced John Locke. The sciences, as we know them, encouraged in

England by the Royal Society formally constituted in 1660, began to emerge after being long in embryo. The change had its impact on the intelligentsia of the Church.

When I touched on John Ray in my opening chapter, I alluded to Dr Derham. A contemporary of Ray, his career, although unique among the Essex clergy, exemplifies the wide diffusion of the new spirit of inquiry. Unlike the others I have so far paraded here, for him the signs and wonders lay in the natural order, and his life was one of unbounded curiosity.

William Derham was born in 1657 near Worcester, six years after Charles II had been defeated there and taken refuge in the oak. He went to Trinity at Oxford and was ordained in 1682. After a spell in Berkshire, he came to Upminster as its rector in 1689. Its population was then only 300 or so, and he was to stay here tranquilly until his death forty-six years later. 'He was strong, healthy and amiable, and he served his parishioners in their bodily as well as their spiritual ailments, few of them requiring another physician during his lifetime.' In 1702 he became a Fellow of the Royal Society; in 1716 a Canon of Windsor; and in 1730 Doctor of Divinity. Although he lived in a then sequestered place, he knew and corresponded with a gifted circle, including Newton, Wren, Sir Hans Sloane and, above all, Ray, of whom he wrote a biography, and edited several of his works and his *Philosophical Letters*.

Derham's interest in the natural sciences was encyclopaedic and often took unusual turns. In 1708 he wrote *An Account of a Child's Crying before Birth at Hornchurch*. He even tasted earwax! 'I could never distinguish any sweetness in it – but think it insipid mixed with bitterness.' He put the Whispering Gallery in St Paul's to a personal test, the cathedral having been completed in 1710. The famous astronomical clock at Hampton Court, having worked so well for 150 years, became defective, and Derham corrected it. His book *The Artificial Clockmaker*, published in 1696, went to four editions by 1734. He wrote papers on the great storm of 1703, on the habits of insects, particularly the flight of ants, and on bird migration. Gilbert White was acquainted with his research, along with Ray's, admiring 'so curious a

Naturalist' and 'that great Philosopher'. White agreed with Derham that showers of frogs were 'a foolish notion'.

Derham used his church tower as an observatory and from it studied sun-spots. One of his books he entitled *Astro-Theology*. He also carried out experiments in the belfry on acoustics and the velocity of light. One of the first to estimate the speed of sound, he had guns fired off in different parts of Essex, including Foulness, finding the distance by counting the vibrations of a half-second pendulum.

In 1711-12 he gave the Boyle lectures, instituted by Sir Robert Boyle, physicist and chemist, for the 'Proof of the Christian religion, against atheists, and other notorious infidels'. Derham's lectures resulted in his major publication, his *Physico-Theology, or a Demonstration of the Being and Attributes of God from his Works of Creation*. The title was no doubt suggested by those of Ray, and is one of those books which anticipated the teleological approach to nature of Archdeacon Paley, who saw design in the universe as evidence of God's existence. In his lecture notes Derham drew liberally from Ray but there are also references to his own Essex-based observations. He mentioned the fossilized trees dug out when the sea breached the walls at Dagenham and Thurrock. Discussing midges, 'one of the very smallest of all the gnat-kind', he comments that, 'In Essex they are called Nidiots .... These gnats are greedy bloodsuckers; and very troublesome where numerous; as they are in some places near the Thames, particularly in the Breach-waters, that have lately befallen near us in the parish of Dagenham; where I found them so vexatious, that I was glad to get out of these marshes.'

The *Physico-Theology* was enthusiastically commended by the original *Guardian* in its penultimate issue (No. 175, 1 October 1713). 'I do not know,' Steele wrote, 'what Upminster is worth; but I am sure, had I the best living in England to give, I should not think the addition of it sufficient acknowledgement of his merit; especially since I am informed, that the simplicity of his life is agreeable to his useful knowledge and learning.' The review concluded that, 'The author may hope to be rewarded with an immortality much more to be desired, than that of remaining in eternal honour among the sons of men.' But Derham's name has been eclipsed in the place where he lived and ministered for so long. He lies beneath the chancel of his parish church, the spot unmarked. He died at High House, which has gone, by the Bell Inn opposite the churchyard, the rectory then being uninhabitable. Of his children, his eldest was a DD and president of St John's College, Oxford.

For my final character, and one with worthy followers, I move ahead into the nineteenth century, when Non-conformist ardour was again well to the fore.

As a child, there was nothing which gave me a keener anticipation than the prospect of a day at the seaside with my parents, and this invariably meant Southend. Often we went by coach, or charabanc, as we called it then, and the route to the coast was part of the excitement. More than once we passed an austere church with 'The Peculiar People' above the door; I think it must have been at Rochford. No one could ever answer my inevitable question, and it was years before I learned the meaning of the strange-sounding name. When I did, there came the further discovery that the sect who worshipped there was unique and indigenous to Essex, and, moreover, all but confined to the south-east of the county.

The story of this remarkable denomination has been peculiar in more ways than one. The name comes from the Book of Deuteronomy, in chapter 14: 'The Lord hath chosen thee to be a peculiar people unto himself', meaning exclusive and specially singled out to be the elect. The name was adopted by the sect when it originated at Rochford, and its adherents were also peculiar in the eyes of others in the common usage of the word. Their ideas and their lives set them apart as decidedly odd.

Their antecedents were Wesleyan. A minister by the name of Atkin in the Isle of Man rejected the staid Anglican Establishment and, crossing to England, took to itinerant preaching up and down the land. Everywhere he travelled he took a welcome doctrine with him, a dual message: the assurance of holiness, of being in a state of grace, and the certitude of salvation. He eventually arrived at Holborn.

There he was heard by one William Bridge who had been a follower of Wesley. Deeply impressed, Bridge passed on the good news to his friend James Banyard, who had also been a Wesleyan minister but had become dissatisfied.

Banyard was a Rochford shoemaker. Now, full of zeal, he returned to his village to spread his tidings of sure deliverance. Chapel Cottages in North Street mark the site where the new movement began in 1838. Services were also held in the open air in the market-place. Soon the sect was established in Union Lane, and then it acquired the old barracks which, after internal alterations, could seat a hundred. The teaching was carried out to nearby towns and villages.

James Banyard displayed an unlikely charisma. One who knew him closely is on record as saying, 'He was the ugliest man I ever saw. As a young man he had been guilty of all manner of tomfoolery, pulling out his lips like a horse's mouth till he had deformed himself.' His natural audacity served him well once he had been converted. With a powerful, commanding voice, he spoke with authority and in a homely language that common folk could understand. He was elected the first bishop of the Church. Four had been nominated, but the others cast their votes for him, and he then ordained them.

To the original doctrine, a new tenet was to be added. With the support of scripture, particularly the Epistle of St James, the sick were now to be healed by anointing with oil and the laying-on of hands. Many were the cures reported in the homes and chapels of the Peculiars.

The followers of Banyard had to endure widespread hostility which often flared into physical violence. They were regarded with suspicion because they were radically different and aloof, all too often the fate of minorities. Perhaps, too, their very air of total, quiet conviction, was a cause of envy. Rejecting as they did in the early days all orthodox medical aid, members were frequently in court on charges of manslaughter.

There was internal dissension as well. Not many years passed before there was a schism. One of Banyard's children fell ill and he sent for a doctor. His modified belief, in medicine supplemented by prayer, led to his rejection at Rochford as bishop. Although he was deprived of the office, he was left in physical possession of the chapel. When he died, the congregations he had founded were divided on the issue. In time, all were to follow his counsel, while always giving priority to the healing power of intercession.

The Peculiars were noted for their virtuous lives, employers and tradesmen finding them reliable and honest. They were sober and neat in dress, the women conspicuous with black bonnets and the men clean-shaven, wearing bowler hats. One writer described them as 'curiously thoughtful' and with a 'somewhat sanctimonious expression of face'. Services on the Sabbath lasted right through the day, the people taking with them their dinner and tea. All were preachers in turn – ministers had to earn their keep by manual labour – and they were well known for their singing. Worship had a revivalist atmosphere, with much hand-clapping and sudden 'testimonies'. Musical instruments were not at first allowed in the chapels but organs and pianos were later introduced. The great occasion of the year, when so many were brought together, was the gathering at the Corn Exchange in Chelmsford to keep the Harvest Festival.

In the last century the Church of the Peculiar People never numbered more than a couple of thousand regulars; between the wars it was still much in evidence, but the organization is greatly diminished now. Scarfe, writing in his *Shell Guide to Essex*, noted that the sect was 'unexpectedly dormant'. However, a reason why it is not so visible today is their amalgamation with the Union of Evangelical Churches.

Conspicuous in the Dengie hundred, they figured as carriers in the marshland tales of Bensusan, all summed up in his 'Brother Ephraim'. A much-respected bishop in the 1930s, was William Heddle of Southend, who died in 1948, one month short of 102. *Kelly's Directories* for those years listed numerous meeting-places apart from Rochford: at Rayleigh, Tillingham, Steeple (where the chapel was not in use) and Prittlewell, and further afield at Great Baddow, Witham and Ramsden. At Grays a chapel is shown located in Salisbury Road, able to seat 300. The furthest the sect reached out, prior to 1900, was to Canning Town and one place in Kent.

In the long undercurrent history of popular, working-class religion, that of the Peculiar People was a very distinctive episode. Much of their regional success must have been due to their direct appeal to a rural proletariat, estranged from the social order represented by the squire and the parson. The Peculiars had far more in common with the like of 'Domesday' Sedgwick and the Gosfield Seer.

10

Francis Quarles
of Romford and Roxwell

Over the past few decades the face of Romford has rapidly changed beyond all earlier recognition. The hands of the planner and the developer have fallen heavily upon the old market town, and yesterday here is now more shadow than substance.

Having fallen into dilapidation, most of the ancestral properties have gone. Among the earlier victims was the mansion of Stewards which ended its days, I understand, as Romford Hall. This was the capital messuage, or principal house, of a manor which made its first appearance in the records in the reign of Queen Elizabeth. It was held in allegiance to the sovereign by one Marcellinus Halys, and then by his son and heir, being at that time part of the lordship of Havering atte Bower. A few years later in Elizabeth's long reign, Stewards was purchased by James Quarles.

The family came from Northamptonshire and traced their immediate descent from George Quarles, an auditor to Henry VII and to Henry VIII. James was the first of the family to settle in Essex. He, too, served the throne, holding the no mean posts of Clerk to the Green Cloth and Purveyor of Victualling to the Navy. James Quarles had other properties in Essex in addition to Stewards. They included houses and land at nearby Squirrels Heath, Harold Wood, Collier Row and Hornchurch. He also had estates in Barking, Dagenham and Stanford Rivers, with several further afield in Hertfordshire. All these holdings seem to have been on a

Francis Quarles, from an old print

modest scale but it is clear he ranked among the minor gentry. However, the status of the family was not to endure for long.

By the time James died in 1599, his wife had given him four sons and three daughters. Robert, the eldest son and heir, was knighted and, marrying several times, also had three daughters. But the one who was to give the family name a lasting distinction was the 'mild and inoffensive' poet Francis Quarles, the third of James' sons.

Francis was born in the autumn of 1592 at Stewards. After his initial education at a country school, he went to Christ's College, Cambridge, and then on to Lincolns Inn to study law, although he was never to practise. We next hear of him at the age of twenty-one when, in 1613, in the retinue of the Earl of Arundel, he attended the wedding in London of the Princess Elizabeth, daughter of James I, to Frederick, Prince of the Lower Palatinate in Germany. The wedding was held on St Valentine's Day, and Elizabeth was the star of the age. Perhaps because of the day, but certainly because of her beauty, she became known to the nation at large as 'the Queen of Hearts'. Her glittering progress through the City, 'like a passage through the Milky Way', was a social event without equal in Jacobean England. John Donne celebrated the marriage with an *Epithalamion*. Sir Henry Wotton was another who later sang her praises. His poem *On his mistris, the Queen of Bohemia* begins:

> You meaner Beauties of the Night,
> That poorly satisfie our Eies,
> More by your number than your Light,
> You Common people of the Skies;
>   What are you when the Moon shall rise?

There seem to be no details of how it was that Francis came to be at the wedding or how shortly after he went to Heidelberg for four years as cup-bearer to Elizabeth. He must have had a patron in high places, who may well have been Arundel. But the sumptuous, carefree life of the palace there came to an abrupt end. In 1619 Frederick accepted the crown of Bohemia, which set in motion the Thirty Years War. The following year, defeated in battle, he and Elizabeth were driven into exile. Their royalty so speedily melting, they were now a tragic couple. 'The Winter Queen' was to end her days forty-two years later as a pensioner in a house on Drury Lane. It was the very height of irony that she died on the eve of St Valentine's Day.

It is most likely that Francis was a personal witness to the curtain-raiser on these dire events. Back from the scene, he went to Ireland as secretary to the learned Archbishop Ussher, the prelate now remembered for his precise dating of the Creation, which he fixed at 4004 BC. Francis served him from 1626 to 1630, returning home with the outbreak of 'the troubles'. He settled back in Essex, but at Roxwell. From 1639 to the end of his life five years later he was Chronologer to the City of London, an appointment secured at the request of the Earl of Dorset, and once held by Ben Jonson and by Thomas Middleton.

His final days were riddled with care. All his sympathies

were with the Royalists in the Civil War. 'Mild and inoffensive' though he became to a later generation, his support for the traditions of Crown and Church, and in particular his tract *The Loyal Convert*, brought down the wrath of the Parliamentarians upon him. His privacy was invaded. They searched his home, seizing his library and his manuscripts intended for the press.

Francis Quarles was of that species of men who constitute an aristocracy of readers, one of those who 'gathered himself up unto the old things'. His death, it is said, was hastened by the wanton act of vandalism. His wife was later to narrate: 'Whereas a petition full of unjust aspersions was preferred against him by eight men, whereof he knew not any two of them save only by sight, the first news of it struck him so to the heart, that he never recovered, but said plainly it would be his death.' Deprived of the physical presence of his books, and his properties sequestered, he succumbed to a consumption in 1644. In addition to his widow, Ursula, who wrote a brief account of his life, he left behind children by a previous marriage, having had a total of eighteen in all. He was laid to rest in London, in St Vedast's, Foster Lane, a church which went with the Fire and was then rebuilt by Wren.

So much for a bare recital of the salient moments in Quarles' life. But his fame rests on his place, small though it is, among the men of letters in his time; a wine glass, as it were, beside the jugs.

'Now under the protection of that great power which is called Oblivion,' the poetry of Quarles has long been without major notice and out of fashion. His works had become quaint and curious two centuries ago, which commended them to Charles Lamb, who could never resist 'the oddities of authorship'. In his letters to Southey he remarked: 'I am glad you have put me on the scent of old Quarles', and on another occasion enthused, 'I have picked up a copy of Quarles for ninepence.' But when Lamb discovered for himself another Caroline poet, George Withers, whose simplicity was more to his taste, his fervour somewhat waned: 'What wretched stuff are the *Divine Fancies* of Quarles! Religion appears to him no longer valuable than it furnishes matters for quibbles and riddles; he turns God's grace into wantoness.' Lamb was ever suspicious of conundrums in matters of faith. Quarles would have been surprised at such a criticism, for in the preface to his metrical romance *Argalus and Parthenia* of 1629, he wrote: 'I have not affected to set thy understanding on the Rack ... by the mere twitch of wit.'

Lamb did admire Quarles' *Emblems*. This was printed in 1635, with the full title of *Emblems, Divine and Moral*. (In the same year Withers published his own, *A Collection of Emblemnes*, which Lamb thought inferior.) Francis worked on it over a period of two years, much of it being done at Brent Hall, Finchingfield, where his friend Edward Benlowes lived, now an even obscurer figure than Quarles.

Books of emblems, where poems were matched with allegorical pictures, were not then a novelty, the Jesuits having produced a series as meditational aids. Their ancestry goes back into the symbolism of the Middle Ages. The poetry in the *Emblems* of Quarles has been variously called 'affected', 'artificial' and 'crabbed', and a modern writer has gone so far as to damn his lines as 'unctuous doggerel'. Robet Southey was of a different mind. 'They have had,' he wrote, 'a singular fate; they are fine poems upon some of the most ridiculous prints that ever excited merriment; yet the poems, in which the ore almost equals the dross, are neglected, while the prints have been repeatedly republished with new illustrations.' Pope's judgement was the very reverse. In the *Dunciad* he wrote of the *Emblems* as one of those books

> Where the pictures for the page atone,
> And Quarles is saved for beauties not his own.

Francis was a most prolific writer. The very titles of his works tell us his moral preoccupations. His first, in 1620, was *A Feast for Worms* (let someone try to get a book with such a title into print today!), a volume I find referred to as 'a gloomy biblical paraphrase'. Among the others are these: a *History of Samson, Hieroglyphics of the Life of Man, The History of Jonah, Job Militant, Hadessa, or the History of Esther, with Meditations Divine and Moral* and *Barnabus and Boanerges, or Wine and Oil for afflicted souls*. Of his *Enchiridion* it was remarked, 'Had this little piece been written at Athens or Rome its author would have been classed among the wise men of his country.'

The *Enchiridion*, from the Greek for 'handbook', is in four parts or 'centuries', each containing one hundred short essays. It was dedicated to 'the glorious object of our expectation, Charles Prince of Wales', with the hope that it 'may lead him to the civill happinesse of more refined days'. One of the essays, on Charity, warns against rejecting the genuine petitioner because of the false: 'Be not too cautious in discerning the fit objects of they Charity lest a soul perish through thy discretion .... Better two drones be preserv'd than one Bee perish.' The *Divine Fancies*, published some years earlier in 1632, was also dedicated to Charles, although the prince was barely one year old! It rises to the very height of flattery and adulation: to 'the royal budde of Majestie ... Illustrious infant ... the future object of the World's wonder'. With inflated sentiments such as these we can understand why Quarles' opponents came knocking at his door.

None of these works could be found today, except in rare collections. Quarles clings on, though, in modern anthologies with one or two pieces, engaging specimens, if hardly representative of his art, which have escaped the confines of their time.

> The World's an Inne: and I her guest,
> I eate, I drinke, I take my rest;
> My hostesse, Nature, does deny me
> Nothing, wherewith she can supply me;
> Where, having stay'd awhile, I pay
> Her lavish Bills, and goe my way.

The comparison is simple, arresting, and fresh enough, with a telling last line and its sting in 'lavish Bills'. There is also his ingenious word-play *On a Cypher*:

> *Cyphers* to *Cyphers* added, seeme to come
> With those that know not Art to a great *sum*
> But such as skill in *Numeration*, know

That worlds of *Cyphers*, are but worlds of *show*;
We stand those *Cyphers*, ere since *Adams* fall
We are but *show*; we are no *summe* at all;
Our bosome-pleasures, and delights that doe
Appeare so glorious, are but *Cyphers* too;
High-prized *honour*, *friends*, This house: The *tother*,
Are but one *Cypher* added to another;
Reckon by rules of *Art* and tell me, than,
How great is thy *Estate*, Ingenious man?
Lord, by my *Figure*, Then it shall be knowne
That I am *Something*; *Nothing*, if alone;
I care not in what *place*, in what *degree*;
I doe not weigh how small my *Figure* be;
But as I am, I have nor worth, nor *vigure*;
I am thy *Cypher*; O, be thou my *Figure*.

Fuller, who had a penetrating eye for character and quality in men, placed Quarles among his *Worthies*: '... had he been a contemporary with Plato, he would not only allowed him to live, but advanced him to an office in his commonwealth. Some poets, if debarred profaneness, wantoness, and satiricalness, that they may neither abuse God, themselves, nor their neighbour, have their tongues cut out in effect; others only trade in wit at the second hand, being all for translations, nothing for invention. Our Quarles is free from the faults of the first, as if he had drunk of Jordan instead of Helicon, and slept on Mount Olivet for his Parnassus, and was happy in his own invention.'

Francis' son, John, born in 1624, followed his father with the pen. He was with the King at Oxford, bearing arms. With the eclipse of the royal cause, he went to London 'in a low condition' and died there of the plague in 1665. I know of his books solely from their titles. As with his father's, the list is long. For specimens there are *Jeremiah's Lamentations Paraphrased*, *Triumphant Chastity*, *Fons Lachymarum*, *or a Fountain of Tears*, *from whence flows England's complaint* and *Elegies and Divine Poems*. They tell us that the mantle of the father had fallen on the son, but not, it seems, the power of his fancy.

The family lingered on for a while. A quit-rent was being paid for Stewards in 1659, and later the estate was parcelled out into several farms. Another house on the old manorial land, a lodge, for many years took on the name.

There was a Yeldham connection. Elizabeth, the daughter of Sir Robert Quarles, married into the family of Symonds, of many generations there. She died in 1666 and was buried in the parish church. Another, Mary, daughter of William Quarles, Esquire, was also interred at Yeldham in 1692. They remain but names in epitaphs.

Of the end of his line I think Quarles would have relished the words in a sermon of Ralph Josselin, the Puritan vicar over at Earls Colne. The devotional language and sentiments of Quarles' poems, so foreign to our ears, had kinship with the pulpit rhetoric of the age: 'Your Wives, your Husbands, your Sonnes and Daughters, whose departing you so much lament, are but stept aside into their retiring rooms, their cool Summer-parlours, the shady cool Grove of the Grave, to take a little rest by sleep, and when they awake they shall return again'.

There is no place for Quarles in Romford or in Roxwell now; they would not recognize each other. The time for the resurrection of his spirit is not yet.

11

Home from the Sea

I expect many readers must feel as I do when I stop and gaze at a really old house. The thought that comes uppermost to mind is of those who have passed their days within its walls, and the ways in which they have left their imprint on the place, be it a cottage on a modest plot or a residence of style and substance. What secrets, if any, lie behind the windows? What manner of lives have been enacted in those rooms?

Of the numerous houses of old Essex which have had associations with the sea, two of particular historic note are little known to the world at large today. In these quiet, leafy retreats, colourful yarns of the main must often have been told, over many a glass of port, I have no doubt. One was the country seat of a distinguished seaman, an admiral of Nelson's day. The other was owned by the son of an Elizabethan who had been on the first great voyage around the world.

On the edge of Stanway, nearer to Birch than to Colchester, is a house called 'Olivers'. Many years back it was saved from near total dereliction. When Morant described the setting, it had 'handsome gardens, canals and fishponds; and a wood adjoining, cut out into pleasant walks'. What you will see now, in Scarfe's words 'very handsome and secluded', is a house mainly of the eighteenth century, but inside there is evidence of a far earlier date, a fifteenth-century roof-truss. An octagonal, brick dovecote with some weatherboards stands here as well.

Olivers derives its name from a family here in the reign of Henry III. Early in the seventeenth century it came into the

Earl St Vincent

possession of the Eldreds, who were of Suffolk origin. A famous member of this family was the John Eldred, 'eminent merchant and navigator', whose voyage in the *Tiger* to Tripolis in Syria and to Babylon in 1583 can be found in the unabridged Hakluyt, *The Principall Navigations, Voiages and Discoveries of the English Nation*. John, a Turkey merchant, was of Great Saxham, where he built Nutmeg Hall, later destroyed by fire. While sailing to Aleppo he had to negotiate a storm which raged for eight days. He made three voyages in all to the East, returning from the last aboard the *Hercules* in 1588. He lived to be eighty, dying in 1632.

So far as I can learn, his connection with the Eldreds who came into Essex remains unclear. But he was contemporary with Thomas Eldred of Ipswich and his son John. According to Wright, it was this latter John who, 'after residing for a considerable time in foreign countries, came and settled in

Colchester, of which borough he was alderman, and one of the bailiffs in the 7th and 21st years of King James the First.' He bought Olivers but in his later years lived at Little Birch, 'the church of which being ruinous, he and the patroness jointly repaired it'. He died in 1646, at eighty-one, and was buried in the church. When it again fell into ruin, his monument was removed to Earls Colne.

His father, Thomas of Ipswich, was one of the '123 persons of all sorts' who accompanied Cavendish with his fleet of three vessels in his circumnavigation of the globe.

As all the succeeding heirs of John Eldred were christened 'John', I am giving each a number to avoid ambiguity.

John Eldred II of Olivers, a Justice of the Peace and an MP, was also 'a Collector of the Sequestrations for the county' in 1645. In plain terms, this means he was responsible for collecting the fines imposed by Parliament on the estates of Royalists. He died in 1682. John III was MP for Harwich in 1688. He died, aged eighty-seven, in 1717. Two more Johns followed quickly at Olivers, the second of whom was the last of the male line here, dying in 1738 at the early age of thirty-three. All were buried at Earls Colne.

Such, in brief, is the family tree of Olivers. However, we can learn rather more of their presence in the house.

The *Gentleman's Magazine* provides a marvellous if often questionable repository of articles on topography and antiquities. In 1837 there appeared in its pages a contribution on Olivers, signed with the unlikely name of 'Steinman Steinman'. Whoever it was who sported this odd *nom de plume*, for such it must surely be, he had sought permission to view the house while on a visit to Stanway. It was the property at that time of a Rev. Thomas Harrison, who I find was not the incumbent in the parish but an important freeholder there.

> The exterior of the house [the visitor wrote] is in no way striking, save for its fearful state of dilapidation, which tells that in a very few years it will cease to exist. It is a long, low, redbrick pile with modern windows; the room once a library has fallen entirely down, as has a great part of the parapet on one side, and the ceiling of the great dining-room is sustained by two rudely-squared stems of trees placed under its beam.

The house stands on a manor embracing 327a, 2r, 36p [acres, rods, poles].

Over the fireplace in the great dining-room is still preserved that portrait of one of the Eldred family which was engraved at the expense of the Society of Antiquaries for the fifteenth volume of the *Archaeologia*. The worthy here represented is Thomas Eldred, of Ipswich ...

A little further on, the writer mentions two paintings which accompanied the portrait. One of these was of a globe, and beneath was this inscription: 'Thomas Eldred went out of Plimmouthe 1586 July 21, and saild about the whole Globe and arrived againe in Plimmouthe the 9 of September 1588. What can seem great to him, that hath seene the whole World and the wondrous works therein, save the Maker of it and the World above?'

Thomas' personal experiences with Cavendish, also a Suffolk man, were not recorded, although they would have been handed down the years within the family, a precious verbal heritage. The closest we can get is to read the account in Hakluyt, written by Master Francis Pretty of Eye. We can read of what Eldred would have witnessed: the novel sights, the privations, the delights and dangers of the two-year expedition. At the very end, with the shore of his homeland almost in view, the two remaining vessels of 120 and 60 tons were almost cheated of their triumph: 'The 9th of September, after a terrible tempest which carried away most part of our sails, by the merciful flavour of the Almighty we recovered our long-wished port of Plymouth.'

There were many other pictures in the house. One was of a ship, apparently remarkable for its time in having four masts. This, and the painting of Thomas Eldred, was erroneously linked by Morant and others with John Eldred of Ipswich. The arms of the Essex family, totally different to his, and granted to John Eldred I of Colchester in 1630, bore three globes azure. In all, Steinman Steinman saw over twenty portraits. In addition to the painting of the old vessel there was a hunting scene, and on the wall of the landing a 'worsted tapestry representing scriptural subjects in figures as large as life'. He also noted: 'In the sitting-room over the chimney-piece is a very fine original portrait of Cromwell in armour, with truncheon.' There had been other mementos of the Protector here, which gives the name of the house an added significance. The Rev. Harrison told of 'much table-linen with the arms of Cromwell upon it' which had once been there. A large brass medal had also been found, bearing the figure of Oliver on horseback, with a Latin inscription: '*Olivarius Dei Gra. Reip. Angll. Scoti. et Hibernia Protector.*' That the house had Cromwellian connections we know from the public office of John Eldred II. It must also have seen the comings and goings of Fairfax's troops during the siege of Colchester.

So far as I can tell, Olivers has long been bereft of all its splendid heirlooms. Some may have found their way to other rooms in private houses or in galleries, but they have vanished from the spot which gave them their full meaning in the living stream of family tradition.

The second house rich in maritime associations lies thirty miles to the south-west. Close by the village of South Weald, an architectural delight, and off the rolling road to St Vincent's Hamlet and Noak Hill, there can be glimpsed the secluded house of 'Rochetts'. There cannot be many who pass it on their way to the nearby Country Park who are aware it was the rural home of one of our greatest sea captains. Here, for forty years, resided 'Jackey' (John) Jervis, the first and only Earl St Vincent. Having left a mighty stamp upon the national scene, he saw out his days in this corner of Essex as an equally formidable eccentric, 'exercising a kindly hospitality to his friends, and an autocratic, though genial sovereignty over his dependants'.

Born in 1735, his career was long and stormy. (It fills close on twenty columns in the Dictionary of National Biography.) Larger than life, more fearsome than Bligh of the *Bounty*, he was inflexible and stern, an enemy of mutineers and dockyard inefficiency, and a rigid disciplinarian with officers and ratings alike, preferring the former to be unmarried and the latter illiterate. His command was frequently administered with grim humour.

Jarvis' finest hour came off Cape St Vincent in 1797, when with Nelson he shattered the Spanish fleet, a victory which some have claimed could have been followed up with more decisive effect. For this he received the freedom of the City of London and many other towns. The widespread acclamation was sealed with a peerage and title conferred by George III.

Two years later, in broken health, he went into close retirement at Rochetts for some months. Soon, however, he assumed command of the Channel Fleet and was appointed First Lord of the Admiralty. In 1810, no longer the titan he was, he made his final appearance in the House of Lords, and eight years later, very feeble, he wintered in the South of France.

He died in 1823, aged eighty-eight, and in accordance with his wishes was carried to Stone in Staffordshire for burial. As a result of an alleged slight, he had resolved never to set foot into the parish church at South Weald again. The village historian, Canon Fraser, told the story: 'It is true that he used to make all kinds of excuses for his refusal to attend divine worship. The old church was cold and slightly damp. He would therefore say that his poor wounded head was so susceptible of cold, or that his cough was so troublesome, that he would only be a nuisance to the congregation. Yet the real cause was the childish vow which he had made in a moment of wounded pride.' He does seem to have suffered much from draughts and, as a consequence, wore a most curious and conspicuous 'cap' which is displayed in Carbonnier's portrait of him. He wore it constantly about the house and is said even to have slept in it. It has been well described as 'a cross between a bishop's mortar-board and a fish-porter's headpiece'.

His wife had inherited Rochetts from her father, Sir Thomas Parker, Lord Chief Baron of the Exchequer. Jervis spent large sums of money on it. Among the attractions was a new wing, which he ordered while at sea, and a verandah at the back for inclement weather, 'the Admiral's stern-walk'. He insisted it should be completed in six months. The architect, at his wit's end to do it in time, had it constructed of timber and then concealed all within thin bricks. The lake, too, was Jervis' idea. On this he kept a four-oar galley, which on one occasion was rowed in hilarious fashion by a bevy of visiting admirals. He also planted an oak to commemorate Waterloo.

His guests had to be down for breakfast at 6 a.m. sharp, but I wonder if this applied to such notables as George IV and William IV, who came here often before they were crowned, or to Nelson and Lady Hamilton. He posted up a list of regulations in the kitchen, two of which read: 'The servants are allowed to eat and drink as much as they please but nothing is to be wasted. No improper conversation allowed.' Yet he extended his strict regime to himself. He rose at 2.30 a.m. and was in the grounds by four. The first servant who joined him there was rewarded with half a crown.

When Jervis ventured forth, no matter how short the journey, he would travel in a coach and six, with a small military escort. 'As soon as the guests had decided on their plans for the day, a time was fixed for the carriages to be at the door, and if the party were not in the hall, and ready to jump in, the Earl would scold them in such forcible language that it never failed to make a lasting impression. Punctuality at meals was strictly enforced.' His ire was directed not only at the vicar. There was the vexed question of his neighbour's trees. Again we can go to Canon Fraser for the details:

> On the adjoining estate of Weald Hall grew a row of trees which seriously interrupted the view from Rochetts. More than once the Earl had asked Squire Tower, as a favour to himself, to have them removed. But to the Squire every stick of timber was sacred, and he repeatedly refused. The trees grew more and more luxuriant every year, but they had no charm for the poor Earl. He became very unhappy. He could scarcely bear the sight of them, neither could he allow his imperious will to be thwarted. One day he was wandering about his grounds with the Squire's son John, a young naval Lieutenant, when his eyes fell as usual upon the obnoxious trees. He sighed, and looked depressed! Presently, he was heard to murmur, in tones just loud enough to be heard by his companion "There's promotion for anyone who cuts down those trees". Nothing more was said at the time but within a week the trees were down, to the great joy of the Earl who rose with the dawn of day to enjoy the charming prospect. Shortly afterwards the young sailor found the promise realised, and himself "posted". What afterwards became of the trees is not known, but it is evident that one good "post" was made of them.

I find this a good yarn, even though it has an air of gossipy invention. But truth is very often stranger than fiction. I hope the old admiral would not have rejoiced could he have seen the wholesale felling of the plantations at Weald Hall a little over a century later.

Today, the area is again becoming well wooded. Rochetts stays very private and guarded behind tall trees at the end of a long drive lined with horse chestnuts. The entrance, with its decorative nameplate, is modest but impressive, a white gatehouse by its side. Opposite is the folly-like Queen Mary Chapel, standing red-bricked and pinnacled above the road. The name is intriguing, deriving from the undocumented tradition that Mary Tudor heard Mass here at the cottage in the kitchen garden of the Tower family estate.

The fine mansion of Weald Hall has gone. So, too, has that of Dagnams, a mile or so to the west. But the undulating landscape in these parts, remarkably not unduly disturbed by the orbital M25, retains the imprint of its stately past. So near to suburbia, it remains a joy to be discovered.

12

Three Legendary Squires

Of the remarkable characters who gave colour to the Essex scene in the not-so-distant past, there are three who richly deserve to be known by a generation emphatically severed from the old life of the land. They stand among the last robust figures of a rural England now almost gone. Individuals of a rare order, proudly independent and with a passion for their native soil, they fully deserve to rank with Shakespeare's 'happy breed of men'. They had much in common. All three were sportsmen. Each served the community on the Bench; each departed with honour in advanced old age, his faculties intact until the end.

In an earlier chapter I wrote of 'Flemings' in Runwell, just several miles away from where I live. Two houses there, of nineteenth-century date, took the parochial name. It was in one of these that there lived 'everybody's old squire', Thomas Kemble.

Old Runwell Hall is the earlier historically, although rebuilt around 1833. Once 'approached from the high road by a picturesque old chaseway', it had long been a farmhouse and today is the site of a psychiatric hospital. The manor had a distinguished past. One of its owners was a Susanna Tonge, alias Clarencieux (her father being Clarence, herald at the College of Arms), a widow who had it from Mary Tudor, having known the royal favour as first lady of the bedchamber. A later possessor was a citizen of London, Simon Rogers, whose sole claim to notability, it would seem, lies in his being the great-grandson of Mrs Herick of Leicester. He was one of the 142 'which she saw descended from her body'.

The ascent of Sir Claude in 'The Lotus'

The other house, Runwell Hall, was built in 1814 and for the next few years was styled New Runwell Hall. Shortly after it was listed as such by White, it became the residence of Thomas Kemble. In his hands it underwent a major alteration by 1853. It was to remain a Kemble property until well into this century, the last of the family to live here being Miss A.F. Kemble. In the 1930s it was described as 'a mansion of brick, pleasantly situated on an eminence, commanding extensive views'. Such is its appearance today on the A132, just west of Rettendon Turnpike. For some years now it has been an imposing and cavernous pub, and in 1985 took the name of 'The Thomas Kemble'.

Thomas Kemble, the first of our trio, was born in the year of Waterloo, the eldest son of Thomas Nash Kemble. He was educated at Winchester, going on to Oriel, Oxford, to get his BA. He inherited the family estates in 1833 and came to the Hall in his early middle-age. He had already been a JP for Hertfordshire and quickly made his mark on the civic affairs of Essex, becoming a magistrate in 1853, although his name had been on the Commission of the Peace since 1838. He was to serve, too, as a High Sheriff of the county. Nor was it long before he emerged as the leading figure in his parish. One story which demonstrates his pride in the locality is the rescue of the old almsbox long forcibly removed from the church.

His wife, Laura, dining out one day with Archdeacon Mildmay at the Bishop's Palace in Danbury, heard that the box was for sale in Chelmsford. On being told, Kemble drove to the Railway Stables, where it was produced by an ostler, also a dealer in antique items. A note on the bottom, 'Rubbish from Runwell Church', helped to establish its identity. The ostler had got it at a sale of effects which had belonged to the late rector of East Hanningfield. Having bought it, and none too soon, for another man, from Oxfordshire, was showing an interest, Kemble had it replaced in St Mary's. It is there still, oak, hollowed out and bound in iron.

No squire worth his salt ever demurred at hunting, and Kemble was no exception. He was good with the hounds and a rare shot, too, on the marshes. In 1887 he privately circulated his *Sporting Reminiscences of an old Squire, being notes jotted down in a Farming Book, by TK*. (This little book has become an extremely scarce item.) Tompkins in his *Companion Into Essex* repeats a tale from E.A. Fitche's *Maldon and the River Blackwater*. Kemble, he wrote, 'had seen the sky darkened by the passing of wild geese, in a formation some half-mile long by a quarter of a mile wide. He could only compare the noise of their passing to "fifty packs of hounds in full cry". At low water, the same veteran had seen seven acres covered by widgeon, curlew and duck.'

Thomas Kemble died at the Hall in 1903. He was eighty-eight and had contracted a chill which carried him off after a three months' illness. He was buried in November, 'every available spot in the ancient little church and churchyard being occupied by people of all classes'.

His eldest son, Thomas Albert, had died in Paris in 1898, aged fifty-seven. A Justice of the Peace, he was more often abroad than at home, although he usually passed the summer at the Hall. His body was brought back for burial.

Kemble's fourth and youngest son, Captain Horatio Fraser Kemble RN, was to follow closely the lifestyle of the father in his later years. He joined the Navy at thirteen, sailed round the world as a lieutenant and, having taken part in several foreign actions, retired from the service in 1896. He took his father's place as an alderman and, like him, became a JP. Horatio was Master of the Essex Union Hounds for three years. A few months before his fatal illness he, too, was appointed High Sheriff. He died in 1912, at Great Claydons, his home over at East Hanningfield. He was sixty-five and left a son and two daughters.

While Thomas Kemble was flourishing at Runwell Hall, an even more exceptional character was making a home and reputation in a remoter corner of Essex.

Tolleshunt d'Arcy above the Blackwater is one of the most appealing of our marsh-country villages, quiet and full of period houses. The past here feels as close as the sea. A maypole, crowned with a weathervane and hemmed in by two hawthorns, stands at the centre opposite the Queen's Head. The church has much antiquarian interest, with brasses which repay close study. The adjacent Hall has been justly celebrated – and never better so than by Wentworth Day in his *Farming Adventure* – with its moat and bridge, its linenfold and Early Renaissance panelling, its paved hallway and an ancient dovecote.

The Georgian-fronted D'Arcy House has added to all this distinction, linked along the street by a red-brick wall to D'Arcy Cottage, also of Regency design. It has known many residents of local prestige and was the home of the novelist Margery Allingham, the pen-name of Margery Louise Youngman-Carter. She began writing at sixteen, aided and encouraged by her father. Well-known for her detective stories, she also produced two volumes of social history. Her book *The Oaken Heart* has the village for its setting. She died in 1966, her husband following three years later. Judging from his illustration of the village reproduced in the splendid guidebook to the church, he was a fine artist.

But, above all, D'Arcy House was the residence for close on seventy years of a truly memorable doctor and man of rare parts. His life had turned into a fable long before it was over, and that was not to be until his ninety-first year.

John H. Salter was born at Arundel in Sussex in 1841. When, at the age of twenty-three, he qualified as a doctor at King's College Hospital, he chose to take over the practice at Tolleshunt d'Arcy, turning down prospects which most young men in his profession would have found far more attractive. The village, however, was not as rustic as some may have thought it to be. The largest in population of the three Tolleshunts (around 700 souls, which has barely doubled in over a century), it was praised just a few years before he arrived as 'large and well-built ... fertile and salubrious, and noted for the friendly and social intercourse of all classes of its inhabitants'. So it was a good place for an extrovert with country habits to be in.

The doctor settled down in the stylish house, having married a girl he had known from childhood (her loss was deeply felt in 1904), and so began what has been well-called a life 'more than commonly long and more than commonly useful'. Here, while not on call, he built up his stamp collection, painted his dogs and flowers, pursued ornithology – often over the barrel of a gun – and tended an orchard and a garden which was a showpiece. More importantly for us, he kept a monumental diary. Its length is staggering. Begun at the age of eight, it finished up at the very end of his life, filling eighty volumes and running to 10 million words. (An edited version was published by the Bodley Head.)

Dr Salter's crowded life was on an equally daunting scale. His practice often involved long and trying journeys, sometimes requiring several changes of horse a day. He needed, and he had, an iron constitution. His prescription for good health he followed religiously: two meals a day, with a biscuit and a glass of white port at mid-morning; a bath, five hours sleep, and lots of regular hard work. He was a most popular and skilful physician, and it is said that he brought 7,000 children into the world.

He was no stranger to hardship and risks. As a young man he displayed an element of bravado, for on Derby Day in 1862 he lost the use of an eye in a boxing match with a gypsy on the Downs. In later years, he had it replaced with a glass one. A photograph I have seen of him shows him to have been powerfully built.

Always adventurous, his horizons were far wider than his parish – he went ten times to Russia to shoot big game. Once he downed two bears in the company of the Tsar. He also shot wolves by moonlight, and they joined the stuffed bears in his drawing-room. For years he had the shooting rights on Old Hall Marsh, taking his gun there in the winter when he was eighty-six. He records of that occasion that he 'never shot better'. Wentworth Day later had the lease, and now the marsh is in the hands of the RSPB.

Dr Salter had a great love of dogs. A Vice-President of the English Kennel Club, he was to own 2,296, representing over forty breeds, and he won more than 600 prizes. A great favourite was his dog Prince Rupert.

A prominent Freemason and a staunch Tory, he was for many years a Councillor, and a JP from 1888. He left his sporting pictures and natural history collection to the county, eventually to be housed in the Chelmsford and Essex Museum.

His end was not long drawn-out. He became ill in March 1932 and died a month later. He was laid to rest in the little cemetery on the corner of Beckingham Road. A tall and badly weathered stone marks the grave at the far end by the bushes. (Margery Allingham lies here, too, with her husband. Until several years ago her sister lived at D'Arcy House. Now, once again, it is the home of a doctor.)

John Salter's funeral service packed the little church of St Nicholas, the Bishop of Chelmsford giving the address. I do not know if one of his closest friends, old Sir Claude Champion de Crespigny, was there for the last farewell. Doubtless his thoughts went out to the place. Sir Claude himself was approaching the end of an extraordinary life, with but three more years to go. When his time came, there passed the third and perhaps the most compelling of these living legends. It was certainly the most theatrical.

The career of Sir Claude de Crespigny was on so large a scale, full of absorbing incidents and dare-devil escapades, that anything near a full biography would take a book to do it credit. He qualifies as one of Noël Coward's 'mad dogs of Englishmen'. It is difficult to know just where to begin in giving a sketch of such a man, but to start with, his ancestral background is of more than usual interest.

He could trace his line back to an ancient Norman family. More directly, he was descended from the Champions and the de Crespignys who left Fonteney to settle in England, fleeing the religious persecution of the Huguenots after the Edict of Nantes was revoked in 1685. His mother was the second daughter of Sir John Tyrell of Boreham House, the last male representative of the main branch of that ancient family.

Sir Claude wrote two volumes of memoirs. The first, *Sporting Memoirs of Sir Claude Champion de Crespigny, Bart.*, was published in 1896, when he was forty-nine. Fourteen years later he produced a revised and up-dated version, *Forty Years of a Sportsman's Life*. Both are now very difficult to come by, and I am fortunate in having a copy of the latter.

He was born in London in 1847, ten years into the reign of Queen Victoria. He joined the navy when he was thirteen, going to sea in 1862 on the first ironclad, the *Warrior*, and then on another vessel to the North American station. Six years later he transferred to the Army, joining the King's Royal Rifle Corps. At first he was with his regiment in southern Ireland, where his steeplechasing earned him the epithet of 'the Mad Rider'. Then, in 1867, he was posted to India. It was there he acquired his taste for big-game hunting, later to be pursued in Florida, East Africa and Morocco, and while in India he won the equivalent of the Grand National.

With the death of his father the following year he became the fourth baronet of the family. Now having responsibilities at home, 1870 saw his retirement from the Army. However, in a few months, lured by the prospect of excitement, he made his way to the front line in the Franco-Prussian War. Passing through France, where he aroused suspicion as a spy, he saw some action with the crack cavalry of the Saxon Uhlans.

In 1872 he married and for a few years resided in the south of Ireland, and then in Wiltshire at Durrington Manor House. It was during his time in Ireland that he was honoured with a bronze medal of the Royal Humane Society. In his own words, it was 'presented to me at a full-dress parade of troops at Winchester. I cannot deny that the occasion was a proud and happy one to me, though, of course, I was well aware that I did nothing more than any man worthy the name would do when I went into the sea at Limerick after a drowning man. These things, in a slang phrase, are "all in a day's work".' His rescue attempt was successful, unlike his dive later to save a boy in the River Blackwater. He gained his 'great confidence in the water' while in the West Indies.

Shortly after coming to Essex, to Champion Lodge at Great Totham, he laid out a cross-country course around his new home, one mile in length and with six demanding jumps. It was made in less than a week, in March 1881, and became the scene of annual races held there for many years. He quickly acquired a local reputation as an eccentric. Any man who applied to be a servant at his house had to pass the test of boxing with the master. The squire was no mean pugilist and once fought for an hour and a half with a broken finger.

In 1882 he went on a shooting expedition to Albania. Later that year he took up ballooning. His attempt in the summer to make a Channel crossing, in the company of the aeronaut Simmons, came to grief on take-off, resulting in his breaking a leg. Simmons went on with the attempt and landed in Arras, covering 170 miles in just over $1\frac{1}{2}$ hours. Next year, however, Sir Claude scored a memorable triumph. On 1 August, again with Simmons, he rose into the sky from a site by the Maldon gasworks. Later that day, their multi-coloured balloon, *The Colonel*, made of india-rubber and bird-lime, came down in Flushing, having at one point soared to a height of 17,000 feet. This was the first balloon crossing of the North Sea, and they marked it in style with a dinner at the Wellington Hotel in the Dutch town. Sir Claude was awarded a gold medal of the Balloon Society of Great Britain and was given another medal by the Royal Aero Club. He had further aerial adventures in 1910 in *The Lotus*. (Simmons was killed five years after the historic flight. Having ascended from Olympia, he seemingly ran into trouble and crashed in a premature landing at Ulting, not far from Champion Lodge.)

In 1886 Sir Claude aspired to join Stanley in his search for Livingstone. Greatly to his annoyance, he was rejected on the grounds that his knowledge of 'darkest Africa' was inadequate.

The bold baronet was noted for seaborne exploits as well. (His father had crossed the Atlantic in a ninety-ton yacht, the *Kate*.) He taught his sons to swim by throwing them into the Blackwater. He was no stranger to turbulent waters. He sailed from Heybridge to Portsmouth in an open boat, a twenty-eight-footer called the *Star*, and in June 1889 made a dangerous crossing of the Channel with one of his sons. That was the year he volunteered for service in Egypt. While there, acting as a war correspondent for the *East Anglian Daily Times*, he swam one of the rapids of the Nile. He was to canoe in Nova Scotia as well as on the Thames.

But his abiding passion was for horse and hounds. He became a familiar figure on many courses throughout the country. In Essex he frequently raced at Lord Petre's course at Childerditch and, more prestigiously, at Galleywood, the

Chelmsford racecourse. In 1888, while riding for the Essex and Suffolk Hunt Cup at Colchester, he fell twice in a field of five, but went on to finish and to win! He did not care much for racing on the flat, and it was not until he was sixty-seven that he gave up the hurdles.

Many are the tales of his rides with the East Essex Hounds. There is the one of how he took the narrow footbridge then at Springfield Lock, jumping the stiles at each end. His daring pursuit of a fox to Goldhanger Creek is best given in his own words: 'The fox was found in a covert north-west of my home, Champion Lodge, and, running under our window, made for Goldhanger Creek, on the Blackwater, a real good point. There I espied him, crouching on a small salting two hundred and fifty yards or thereabouts from the river wall. Of course the hounds could neither view nor wind him. I accordingly swam out to his coign of vantage, with the whole pack after me. Finder, a big black and white stallion hound I had from Jack Fricker, was first up, and the two leading hounds dropped poor Charlie. I at once proceeded to dive, and after some rather exhausting struggles, recovered his carcass, which the hounds broke up on the salting.'

It can hardly be denied that Sir Claude, a born raconteur, was a boaster, although redeemed by being a genial one. Not for him the light under the bushel, and he could never let slip the chance of an audience. When a marine lake was opened by his wife at Tollesbury in 1907 (reported as the brain-child of Dr John Salter), 'A humorous speech was delivered by Sir Claude de Crespigny, who recited anecdotes of rescues from five feet of water, at which he as a middy had assisted, and alluded to his subsequent swimmings in every continent of the globe.' (It was the occasion, as well, for the laying of a cornerstone of a new parish room, Dr Salter and fellow Masons presiding.)

The shadow of two stark tragedies fell across the ageing squire. Of his five sons, the eldest, Captain Claude de Crespigny, committed suicide at Peterborough in 1910, a revolver found by his side. His career in the Life Guards had been outstanding. He had served in India and was badly wounded in the Boer War while saving the lives of two privates, for which he received the DSO. Like his father, he was a distinguished sportsman, in riding, shooting and polo. The burial was at Champion Lodge, in the family vault in a wood near the park. He was only thirty-nine. Another son, Captain Claude Norman de Crespigny, was killed in action on the Western Front at Compiègne in September 1916.

As Sir Claude moved into his final years, he could not be so dashingly active. Walking became his chief delight and exercise. A touch of the old self-display remained. At sixty-three, he walked from the Lodge to the Grand Hotel in London for a bet of half a crown.

He was a magistrate and also a Deputy Lieutenant for the county in 1933. He was then eighty-six. Unlike Kemble and Dr Salter, he had no taste for politics, though he had indulged in a short flirtation. 'Upon settling down in Essex,' he wrote, 'one of the first matters to which I turned my attention was, of all things in the world, party politics! This was the first (and I hope it may be the last) time in my life that I took my share in the dull game of politics.'

In June 1935 the end came to 'one of the hardiest and pluckiest men in England', as an Essex contemporary truly called him. His heir, Raoul, the second of his sons, succeeded to the baronetcy. Towards the end of the First World War he had commanded the Brigade of Guards. He died in 1941. The sixth baronet, Sir Henry, died five years later.

The name 'Champion Lodge' has gone. The Victorian house, however, survives as Totham Lodge and has become a nursing home, secluded among trees at the far end of a narrow lane which also leads to Home Farm. There are no male descendants of the line now, but a Colonel Lancaster married a de Crespigny. At the time of writing, she is in her eighties and resides in Northamptonshire.

The memory of Sir Claude and his celebrated family has all but faded in the locality. There are three farms, called de Crespigny Herds, at Great Totham, Bocking and Stisted, but no pub or street commemorates the illustrious name. That this can happen in only half a century I find depressing. It has been the fate, as well, of one of Sir Claude's outstanding predecessors in the great sporting squire tradition: Sir Henry Bate-Dudley of eighteenth-century fame at Bradwell juxta

Mare. Surely the time is well overdue to provide some visible reminder of their commanding presence in these neighbourhoods, as has been done for Thomas Kemble at his Hall in Runwell.

13

The Saga of the Honywoods

Of all the old gentry who acquired estates in Essex from outside, there can be few to rival in interest the long line of the Honywoods. Their residence in the county is a continuously absorbing tale, their public roles and private lives full of incident and colour. Unlike the histories of so many landed families, the Honywoods' is far more than solely a roll-call of names.

The first of the family to come from their seat in Kent settled at Marks Hall or Markshall, one mile north-west of Coggeshall. In this tiny parish, barely 800 acres in extent and one of the most diminutive in Essex, his descendants stayed for close on three centuries. In 1831 the population was only fifty-two, over a half being Honywoods and their retainers. The golden days there have long been over, as I shall subsequently show. The fine house, the wooded park, the little church of which they were the patrons, has each in melancholy turn been effaced.

The Honywoods began their days in Kent, 'where they flourished soon after the Conquest'. They were at first 'de Honeywood', taking their name from a village called Hunewood or Henewood. One of them in the Middle Ages married the daughter of a nobleman, 'the capital seat of whose baroncy was Billericay or Court-up street, in Allington near Honywood'. (I mention this as given by Wright for its no small topographical interest. This was one of the three Billericays in England, only one of which, that in Essex, has endured as a place-name. It also continues to defy all attempts at scholarly explanation).

The fortunes of the family grew through various

Dame Mary Honywood, from an original portrait

well-connected marriages, and a number held high office, military and civic, including a baron of the Cinque Ports and a Lord Mayor of London. The parent stock of those at Markshall are mainly shadowy figures now. Few emerge as people from the medieval family tree. But the annals of the Honywoods from the middle of the sixteenth century read like the narrative of a cavalcade, opening with a flourish to bring the remarkable Mary Honywood née Waters upon the stage.

Robert Honywood bought 'Merkshall' in 1605. He was sixty, and the size of his family had determined the move, having had fifteen children by two wives. His father was dead, but to his new home he brought his mother, Dame Mary.

She had been a rich heiress and had married Robert Honywood the Elder of Charing in Kent. All her brothers, by tradition ten, had perished in a single visitation of the plague. This is only the first of those prodigious numbers which were to mark out her life for the notice of posterity. She gave birth to sixteen children, of whom only three were not to reach maturity. Robert was her eldest. The last-born son, Captain Isaac, was slain with most of his men at the Battle of Newport in 1600. Dame Mary lived on to her ninety-third year, the matriarch of the family, and was laid to rest beside her husband in Kent, at Lenham. She could be said to have founded a dynasty, for by the time of her death 367 persons were descended from her! In addition to the sixteen children of her own, 114 were grandchildren, followed by 228 in the third generation, and nine in the fourth. This achievement was inscribed on her monument placed in the church at Markshall but can now be seen in the south chapel of St Peter-ad-Vincula at Coggeshall.

There is more to her life than taking the palm for offspring. She was a strict Calvinist and most exacting with herself, haunted by the doctrine of predestination. As Mary Waters, in her twenties she witnessed the martyrdom of John Bradfield at Smithfield, pressing so close to the fire that the shoes were trodden from her feet. She had to walk barefoot back into the City. Bradfield, one-time minister at Saffron Walden, was apprehended in 1554, at the same time as John Rodgers.

In the time of that short-lived but fierce persecution, which has stamped the reign of Mary Tudor for ever as that of 'Bloody Mary', Robert Honywood's mother-to-be used to visit the prisons 'to comfort and relieve'. But she was to develop an agonizing spiritual malady, consumed with doubts about her salvation, like that other great Puritan lady just a few years later, Mary Rich, Countess of Warwick, away across country at 'Leez'. The doubts of Mary Honywood reached cancerous proportions. Foxe was one of those who tried to allay her fears, and Thomas Fuller in his *Worthies* narrated the story with its dramatic twist and conclusion. He had the details from the Bishop of Durham, who had heard it from Mary's own lips. In vain did Foxe argue with her. There came the moment when she raised a Venetian glass and, hurling it to the ground, cried out, 'I am as surely damned as this glass is broken!' Fuller wrote:

> Here happened a wonder, the glass rebounded again and was taken up whole and entire. I confess it is possible (though difficult) so casually to throw a brittle a substance that, lighting on the edges it may be preserved, but happening immediately in that juncture of time, it seemed little less than miraculous. However, the gentlewoman took no comfort thereat (as some have reported and more have believed) but continued a great time after (short is long to people in pain) in her former disconsolate condition without any amendment. Until at last, the great Clock-Keeper of Time, who findeth out the fittest moments for his own mercies, suddenly shot comfort like lightning into her soul; which once entered, ever remained therein ... so that she led the remainder of her life in spiritual gladness.

Her cure has that feature of a releasing 'trigger' so often to be found in the literature of sudden, new-found grace.

One of the treasures at Markshall was a portrait of Dame Mary. According to Wright, this was done in 1597, when she was seventy, showing her in a widow's garb and with a book in her hand. It hung for generations in the dining-room. However, this does not match the portrait purchased from the house by Colchester Council. In this ancient painting she is depicted in front of a curtain, hooded and draped in black. Her face looks out above a ruff. Yet she holds no book. Instead, beneath her outstretched right hand with the forefinger pointing, there is within an ornate, painted frame the very wording to be read upon her monument. Unless there were two portraits of Dame Mary, the memorial in the picture may have been grossly mistaken for a book. Wright also affirms that on her hat could be seen

'Aetatis Suae 70' and on the opposite side 'Anno Dni. 1597'. In the photograph I have seen, admittedly a darkened reproduction, this is certainly not apparent.

Her son Robert enlarged the house and added a new front. His initials were carved on the oak chimney-piece in the hall, with the date 1609. Either then or later, quarterings from the family coat of arms were placed above the entrance. Despite these and subsequent alterations the mansion kept to the end much of the ancient structure built by the Markshall family who had been granted the manor in the twelfth century and who continued to live there to the reign of Elizabeth.

Robert died seven years after his mother. He was eighty-two. Married twice, by his first wife he had twenty children. He lost Isaac, one of his boys by her, at the siege of Maestricht, while another served as a captain in the Low Countries. His eldest son by this marriage, Sir Robert, was steward to the 'Queen of Hearts' in Bohemia, her 'honest and faithful Robin', and I wonder if he encountered Quarles there. He supported the King, Frederick, in the Wars of the Palatinate, serving as a colonel. 'In this service he sacrificed a great part of his patrimony.' He returned to England but went abroad again, to Holland, when the Civil War broke out. After the execution of Charles I he came back to his homeland. It would seem he was no longer overtly Royalist in his sympathies, for he became a member of the Council of State in the year before the Restoration and was Ambassador to Sweden.

In his last years he eased his darker hours by translating an Italian book, the biography of a Venetian, into English. He dedicated the volume to a brother-in-law, in which he wrote, 'I began this in the circumstances of an uncomfortable old age and ruined fortune, brought upon me rather by public calamity than private vice.' He had sixteen children.

His father's second wife bore six sons and a daughter. The eldest son and heir, Thomas, was knighted in 1632. A leading Parliamentarian in the county, he commanded one of the three Essex regiments for Cromwell. With 2,000 volunteers assembled at Coggeshall, he marched to join Fairfax for the siege of Colchester. After the town had been taken, he was entrusted with dismantling its defences. He did not carry out his orders, however, and no disciplinary action was taken against him. He was also at the Battle of Worcester. On his way back home he was awarded a doctorate of Civil Law at Oxford. After representing Essex in the Commons, he sat in the Protector's House of Lords. He died aged eighty at Westminster but was taken for burial to Markshall.

The Honywoods' reputation for longevity continued. The wife of Sir Thomas lived to be seventy-five. She was noted for her piety, kindness and penetrating mind. Her son, Peter, reached the most advanced age of ninety-six. The youngest boy, John Lamotte Honywood, was three times an MP for Essex. He was the great-grandson of Francis la Motte, a Flemish settler from Ypres who was an elder of the Dutch church at Colchester in 1570.

The life of John Lamotte came to a sad and bizarre end, as Sir John Bramston tells us in his memoirs:

> He had married the sole daughter of Sir William Wiseman, of Rivenhall, and having no child, she prevailed with him to settle his whole estate on her by a trick, that is, by telling him King James was certainly returning [i.e. James II, from exile] and then his estate would be confiscated, and therefore advised him to settle his estate on her: which having done, he grew very sad and discontented in mind, attempting to choke himself by thrusting the rump of a turkey down his throat; another time he got tobacco-pipe ends into his mouth; and once he attempted to throw himself down stairs, but was prevented in all these. Yet his discontent still continued, and his wife had two men that attended him; but he after a while dissembled, so that she, being miserable to baseness, for thrift, put one off, and, it seems, thought herself and one man might guard him well enough; but on Sunday the 14th of January, 1693, his wife going out of the chamber, he sent the man to fetch him a glass of small beer from the tap: he took an old broken garter, fastened it to the curtain-rod of his bed, and hanged himself, by the assistance of the devil, for both the garter and curtain-rod else could not have held a quarter of his weight.

The next in line at Markshall was Sir Thomas' son Robert, another soldier and MP for the county. When he died he was followed by his son Richard. He, too, had a boy called Richard, who would have inherited had he not died very young. But it is Robert's brother, Sir Philip, who steals the limelight at this point. He continued the tradition of military service. First commissioned in 1694, he was a captain in the Royal Fusiliers. He saw action in Flanders some while later. Then, as Colonel of the First Dragoon Guards, becoming known as 'Honeywood's Dragoons', he showed great bravery in three engagements in Portugal. In 1710 he became a Brigadier-General. But a drinking spree with fellow officers led to a temporary downfall.

Swift, in one of his letters to 'Stella', provides the details. Sir Philip, 'drinking a glass with one hand and discharging a pistol with the other', indulged in a tirade against the new administration in London and the Tory Chancellor Harley in particular. Philip put up a lame defence but was forced to resign. When the Whigs came back to office, he was again given a commission. In the Highland rising of 1715 he was wounded in the shoulder while in Lancashire. Three years later he had his portrait done by Kneller. Further service at home and abroad culminated at the Battle of Dettingen in 1742, where George II was the last British monarch to take the field. In a letter to Sir Horace Mann the following year, Horace Walpole wrote: 'Honywood's regiment sustained the attack, and are almost all killed: his natural son has five wounds, and cannot live.' Colonel Sir Philip Honywood, the senior General of Horse and Field Marshal, came back to receive the Order of the Bath. He died at Greenwich in 1752 and was buried with full military honours at Portsmouth, of which he was Governor. If there was a memorial there, no trace of it has been found. He died unmarried.

With the decease of young Richard, his uncle, a second Colonel Philip, came to the fore at Markshall. He, too, had been at Dettingen, coming away with twenty-three wounds and a silver plate in his head. Before he began his service life abroad, he had contracted a marriage with a young heiress. It was not a success, each finding the other unattractive, and they parted – which brings us to a curious tale. When Philip returned to England, he went to take the waters at Bath, where the master of ceremonies drew to his notice a beautiful woman who bore the same surname as the Colonel. She proved to be none other than his estranged wife! She must have strikingly improved with age and separation, for there followed a reconciliation, and the marriage contract was renewed, and publicly announced, in 1751.

It was at Bath that the General, as he rose to be, became acquainted with Thomas Gainsborough. This resulted in a celebrated equestrian portrait. It shows the General mounted on his favourite charger, sword upright in hand, against a lush background of oaks and silver birches. George III coveted the painting but it was to remain in the family for long after. Today it is in the USA, where it went for £4,500 some years ago.

The glory of the estate was in its trees, in both the deer park and the surrounding woods: great sentinel oaks, elms, larches, beeches, Scots firs and silver birches by the lake. In will after will the clause appeared 'impeachable of wilful waste in felling timber'. The General's will, which runs to eight sheets of parchment, laid down the condition that any of his successors who cut down the trees, apart from the need of necessary repairs, or who failed to take the name of Honywood within twelve months of inheriting, would forfeit the estate.

He was MP for Appleby in Westmorland for thirty-one years, having property there. He was deeply affected by the death of his only son. His own end came at his town house in Berkeley Square in 1785. He was in his seventy-fifth year. His wife followed him a few months later. They were buried in the church at Markshall which is shown on the map he had commissioned in 1765. A later, tithe-award map of 1842 gives the layout of the gardens, with the chapel, an ice-house, dog-kennel, deer-leap and brick kiln.

With no heir in the direct line for the first time in 200 years, Markshall was left to a distant cousin. This was Filmer Honywood. He died a bachelor in 1809, a mere sixty-four. The days when the family could boast that its members lived long in the land were almost over. One of them about this time, Fraser Honywood, the banker, stipulated in his will that all who were his kin could claim a legacy. Four hundred came forward as relatives of himself and his father!

Filmer was sent to Parliament three times by Kent. His epitaph included these words: 'He was a Whig of the old school, having to his utmost opposed those measures that separated America from this country, and the same destructive system that brought on the present ruinous war with France, so fatal to all Europe.'

The next to inherit was William Honywood. He had fought in America, retiring from the army when the peace was signed in 1783. He, also, was a staunch Whig, holding his political creed right through his life 'with unshaken perseverance and incorruptible fidelity'. He was the squire at Markshall for only thirteen years, passing away at the age of forty-one. He left three sons under the guardianship of his wife Priscilla, an Essex woman, and their great-uncle, the Rev. Philip Honywood. The parson was a character, a great hunter with the beagles until frailty laid him low. His brother-in-law commissioned a painting of the dogs, which survives in private hands. His hounds were sold to Prince Albert.

Of the three sons, William Philip excelled as a sporting man and excessively so, a hard drinker but never seen drunk. He had a passion for the races at the Galleywood course in particular where he instituted the Marks Hall Stakes. His death was brought on by a chill. With no children, he left the estate to an infant godchild. His brother Robert was deeply in debt to the tune of at least £12,000, and William had said of him, 'If I left Marks Hall to Robert there would soon not be a stick or stone left belonging to a Honywood ... the Jews will have it in six months, and there will not be a timber-tree left.'

A long and complex legal wrangle ensued, but the widow, Mrs Frances Emma Honywood, was left undisturbed. She was faced with heavy costs from litigation, and receipts from the land were falling. By her order, the church, which stood only yards from her threshold, was demolished in 1875. St Margaret's was rebuilt in brick, an unprepossessing hexagonal church. Mrs Honywood died twenty years after, somewhat unexpectedly, it was reported. Robert and her other son, Walter, had pre-deceased her.

The ancient connection was finally and ignominiously

broken. The great estate of over 2,000 acres was sold for £17,500. It went to Mr Price, the notable candle-manufacturer. The venerable trees were mostly axed, and the timber went for £12,000. Only a few stand now along the drive, and one is thought to be 700 years old, a last witness to a fabulous longevity.

Everything in the house went up for auction: rare books, prints, plate and china, and a host of portraits, a vivid commentary on 300 years of family life. The paintings included three Lelys, one by a pupil of Van Dyke, and another by Sir Godfrey Kneller. Well over twenty members of the family, relatives and friends, once looked down from the walls. Oliver Cromwell had pride of place over the oak fireplace in the great hall, and there was a portrait of Fairfax nearby.

In 1932 Mrs Price the third looked out on a park of 200 acres stocked with fallow deer. But in the spring of that year the penultimate deprivation was committed. There was no longer the umbilical pull of a distinguished name and romantic past. She disliked the church and so had it pulled down. Some monuments were saved in the nick of time, removed to Coggeshall and to Colchester. The others were buried in the vault, consigned to the stokehole, and the site was covered in rubble. They await an archaeological Last Judgement.

Then came the war. An air-base was built which encroached upon the park. The fence was broken and the deer escaped. Mrs Price moved out and the mansion became a headquarters of the USAF. When hostilities were over, it was occupied by a horde of squatters. The vandalism was so extensive that it was judged beyond restoration. And so the house came down in 1951.

There remains the fate of the 'miraculous' glass, thrown from the hand of Dame Mary in despair. In a footnote in T.W. Davids' *Annals of Evangelical Nonconformity in Essex* (1863), he remarked 'The glass, unhappily, was broken some time since', which seemed to imply it was no more. However, it has been a delight for me to learn that, although damaged, this premier heirloom of the family has survived.

Again, the pages of the invaluable *Essex Review* come to our aid. Gurney Benham, writing there in 1933 on the Honywood memorials and the cup, tells how he traced its whereabouts. It was then in the possession of Mr Robert Hall-Dane, a lineal descendant of Mary, residing in County Wexford, Ireland. In the article, a photograph appeared, the first ever taken. (Hall-Dane was descended from the posthumous child of Sir Thomas, the sole heir in blood. A girl, she was christened 'Matthew', so great was the disappointment at her sex.) The cup is described as being dull yellow in colour and seven inches high. It could have been made by a Venetian who set up a factory in London in 1574; he had a patent for making drinking-glasses in England. Late in the nineteenth century, the glass was 'mischievously broken', and a silver stem had to be added to keep it in one piece. Silver side-pieces are also a later addition. I understand it now lies in obscurity in an Irish bank, where hopefully it will long enjoy safe-keeping, one of the last physical links with a spectral past.

Marks Hall has almost lost its identity. There are contemporary maps which do not show it, and as an ecclesiastical parish it has been absorbed by Coggeshall. It seems on the way to sharing the fate of Hunewood, where the long story of the family began. Two lakes remain, said to have been dug by Cromwellian soldiers in the final days of the Civil War.

The Honywoods had two mottoes, the second of which can set the seal upon the remains and records of their history: '*Moriendo vivo*' – I live by dying.'

14

Pubs Lost and Found

I am one of those who feel the lure of pubs, and not solely for a pint of ale. Much of our legacy from the past can be found in houses of call, as well as the character of the localities they serve. They are an inherent feature of the land in town and country alike, a part of our image of England.

Frame in your mind the archetypal village, and one pub at least with its sign is standing there. Where they have gone, and there is many a rural retreat which lacks them now, there is for me a sense of diminution, the loss of a visible and social focal point. The older give an air of continuity and endurance. Close any one of these and remove its name, and yet another doorway is closed on all our yesterdays. Amid ever-changing fortunes and the ups and downs of status, the inn or tavern has had a central role in the history of the people. It is a unique institution, as foreigners who come here well appreciate, and for long was the twin pole with the parish church in the life of the community. Yet the local can still be said to be *the* place where two worlds meet and intermingle, a special 'brew' of the public and the private. The elitist circle of the coffee morning is no fair substitute for that.

The pull of the pub has taken me to many here in Essex but, *Deo gratias*, they are only a fraction of those which remain to be seen and savoured.

Here, then is a varied selection of those I have found down the years, through visitation and that ally of all exploration, reading. I include some which are dear departed. So many pubs have gone, which gives them a special aura of fascination. Defoe wrote of Brentwood, Ingatestone and

'The Cats' at Woodham Walter

Chelmsford as 'full of good inns', while Ogilby in his *Traveller's Guide* of 1699 said the same of Stratford and Kelvedon. All these places, it is worth noting, are on the Roman highway from London to Colchester. The pages of White's *Essex* of 1848 reveal just how many 'good inns' there were in these then major staging-posts. For Stratford, the gateway to Essex, he lists twenty inns and taverns.

Brentwood had eleven, including the Railway Hotel, built with the opening of the line in 1846. Ingatestone with Fryerning had eight. The Woolpack there has since become the Huntsman. Chelmsford could boast forty-six, most being in the centre of the town. The borough of Colchester with its sixteen parishes had a grand total of ninety, the vast majority in the town itself, and sixteen alone on the High Street. The Bishop Blaize here became the Locomotive in 1843, the new landlord being a retired engine-driver.

These figures do not include a host of humbler beerhouses. These proliferated after being encouraged by legislation in the reign of William IV, the reason for so many pubs adopting that monarch's name. Yet, impressive as these statistics are, they certainly mark some reduction in premises compared with the previous century.

One or two further indications of the scale of the trade in former times will suffice. In 1789 there were eighteen inns in Epping town, including Epping Place which ceased to be an inn a few years later. In the High Street, the White Hart went just over twenty years ago. Built in 1896, it replaced the old White Hart which had been pulled down. In the seventeenth century this had been the Cucking Stool (from the privy stool used to duck scolds) and then the Greyhound. Grays Thurrock, too, could once show a prodigious number, and was said to have more than any other town of comparable size in England. With a population of barely 1,500 in 1848, it then had only six licensed houses. It had ceased to have a corn market, being rivalled by Romford, and this may, in part, explain the decline in its taverns. The predominant trade was brick and tile manufacture, linked with the quarries. Although steamers plied to Gravesend five times a day, its maritime status had long ago diminished. Only one pub name reflected this association, the Sailor's Return. There is a Ship and a Wharf Inn in the town today. In 1848, as well, there were sixteen public houses in Witham and fourteen in Coggeshall.

So much for a few telling figures. What was more noticeable to the keen observer towards the end of the nineteenth century was the disappearance of pictorial signboards. Miller Christy in his still unrivalled *Trade Signs of Essex* lamented that their golden age was over. In his day, in Epping High Street ten boards could be seen 'all swinging over the pavement in the ancient style', but only one, that of the *White Horse*, bore an image. He found the great majority of Essex pubs had signs which were scripted only. That was in 1887. I doubt if this is so today, for pictorial boards have for some decades been coming back into fashion.

Nor can it be said that most of our pubs are tippling houses for manual workers, as they were in the trade slump between the last of the coaches and the rise of the motor car. They are frequented by people right across the social spectrum. The development of the saloon bar to attract a middle-class clientele has ensured that. Yet I know a few pubs in outlying spots which I am glad to say keep something of a proletarian character, with homely rooms and the saloon often akin to a parlour. These have not yet succumbed to pressure from the brewers or to the current taste to go 'up market'. There were formerly two of these in my own village of West Hanningfield, an appropriate place to begin my peregrinations.

The Ivy House has gone, replaced by a modern residence which keeps the name. Only a few in the parish can remember it now, elderly folk who recall that it brewed and sold its own beer. In the 1920s it was kept by a Mrs May, who must have been related to Joseph May, sexton, beer-retailer and shopkeeper in the 1890s. David Smith in the absorbing history of his own family, *No Rain in Those Clouds* (Dent, 1943) mentions him several times. He was known in the village as 'Bryant' May. He worked part time at Link House Farm, owned today by Michael Gray of Gray & Sons. No longer brewing at Springfield, Michael Gray and his mother are prominent figures in the Essex trade with their ownership of fifty distinctive pubs.

The other house on my home ground, a little way out from the centre, is a cottage with a charming wayside garden. This is now Garden Cottage (late Willow Villa) but was formerly the Plough. I have never found it listed as such but a previous owner showed me a photograph from an old *Farmers Weekly* (of around 1910, if I remember right) in which draymen can be seen unloading their barrels outside.

The tiny tap-room, long since converted to modern use, retains a separate identity.

To my discovery that this was once a pub, I can add a cautionary tale. It will demonstrate the pitfalls in the quest to elucidate the meanings of obscure and obsolete names.

Nearby is Elm Farm, the home until his death several years ago of Mr Ralph Stacey, retired farmer and one of a family who have worked the land in the Hanningfields for nigh on a century. With his invalid wife, we had many a good conversation in his timbered living-room. The house, which was in a bad way, has since been sold; restored and largely transformed, it now looks very important in the landscape.

Incidentally, Ralph's mother, Elizabeth, who ran the farm after her husband's death, seems to have been a formidable lady. Strictly 'chapel', she set up a Sunday school in the parish. She also had no truck with drinking. Once, Ralph told me, she marched across to the barn where a party was being held and up-ended a cask of ale, which I presume had been smuggled in.

There came a moment in such engaging talk when he mentioned in passing 'the Jerry field'. This was opposite what had been the Plough, and he suggested, with a wink, that he thought it took his name from customers relieving their bladders there! I did not question this but held my tongue, convinced that, as a budding local historian, I had found the answer which his naming of the field confirmed. On a map of the parish, dated 1805, there is land at nearby Helmons on the Green marked the 'Rev Doctor Mills'. When I followed this up in manorial court records, I learned that Dr *Jeremiah* Mills was a Doctor of Divinity and Dean of Exeter Cathedral. So that clinched the origin of 'Jerry' here, or so I confidently thought. It was only some time later that I had to change my mind – and on two counts. In 1805 the two fields, as they were then, opposite the Plough were in the name of a Mrs Phelps. More importantly, I came across the once widespread use of the expression, 'Jerry shop'.

Tom and Jerry were two 'bloods' in a very popular book last century, *Life in London, or the Day and Night Scenes of Jerry Hawthorn and his elegant friend, Corinthian Tom.*

Published in 1821, it was written by Pierce Egan, a sporting journalist with a particular interest in pugilism. *Life in London* depicted the pastimes of the capital in the Regency period and was illustrated by the satirical cartoonist George Cruikshank. Tom and Jerry frequented low haunts in their escapades, and from this it has been surmised that their names were taken up as the sign for an alehouse of the more common sort. According to the *NED*, a 'Tom and Jerry' was some kind of mixed beverage. Whatever its precise origin, very soon a Tom and Jerry shop became abbreviated to a Jerry shop or house, synonymous with a beershop or small tavern. The expression is now defunct, except for the cartoon cat and mouse, of course.

In the opposite direction to my home there was such a Jerry house on the Galleywood road in Great Baddow. The cottage is still there, weatherboarded and showing its age at Pipers Tye. This was the Found Out (named by Christy as the New Found Out) and remained in business until well into this century. It is not mentioned in White, but it could have been one of the beerhouses he gives by owners. If it was, it later grew to full pub status.

Also in Great Baddow was a brewery in Church Street. The buildings remain, the largest a furniture showroom, while the others are used by antique dealers etc. Essex Radiators Ltd have that which was a depot for soft drinks. The brewery was a family business, run by the Crabbs, the first of whom came to Baddow in 1798. It passed to his son, Richard Crabb, who had it for over seventy years. It then went to Richard Hatley Crabb, very much a local personality and a great planter of trees. His death in 1899 signalled the brewery's demise as well, his three sisters being ardent supporters of the Temperance movement. Elizabeth Stacey must have been pleased at that!

Another former brewery can be seen in north Essex, at Wethersfield. Long in disuse, it stands in the grounds of the Brewery Tavern. According to William White, there were four taverns here and six beerhouses.

Many pages could be filled on the ancient pubs of Chelmsford. Several were of prime importance, standing in key positions. The Saracen's Head, facing the Shire Hall, reached its heyday in the 1700s. With many alterations down the years, particularly to the façade, it is far older than it looks. It used to be distinguished by a pictorial sign, if Joseph Strutt's novel *Queenhoo Hall*, published in 1808, can be relied upon – that of the Saracen or Man Quintain. Trollope is reputed to have stayed at times at the Saracen, although he does not refer to it in his autobiography. As I write this, the spacious house is boarded up, its future uncertain. In recent years it has gone down in the world, no longer the place it was when it ranked as the foremost hostelry in the county town. I hope it will not meet the fate of that in Chesterton's colourful fiction, 'destroyed by lemonade'.

> The Saracen's Head looks down the lane,
> Where we shall never drink wine again,
> For the wicked old women who feel well bred,
> Have turned to a tea-shop the Saracen's Head.

At the other end of the High Street, on the corner of Springfield Road, stood the rival Black Boy. A print of 1762 shows it well. The sign of a black boy, traditionally used to denote the premises of a tobacconist, hung from a massive timber projecting over thirty feet from the house and was supported by a vertical one not much shorter, the whole frame allowing free access along the thoroughfare. In the print, a procession of judges with attendants and a coach is depicted passing beneath it. It must have been a rarity even then, for legislation had meant the end of most signs over roads as a public nuisance. The emblem of another inn almost opposite is also shown in the print, suspended in a magnificent wrought-iron frame on a tall, free-standing pillar. The Lion, which by around 1900 was the Queen's Head, was owned by the Baddow brewery. A photograph of that date shows there was no sign then, and the site of the pub is now filled by shops. It was at 'the Lyon' in 1543 that a stranger was drowned 'by misfortune and his own lewdness', while two years later the parish registers inform us that 'Wyllyam Pemberton, servaunte to the Irle of Essex, was slain at the Lion by one of his Fellows'.

The Black Boy was Tudor in origin. A deed of 1642 shows

it had earlier names: the Crown, the New Inn and the King's Arms, this last name probably from the room known as 'the sheriffs prison' which displayed the royal insignia. The first known reference to the inn by its later title appears in the church register for 1612, where it is written 'the Black Boye'.

In the Chelmsford Museum there is a wooden boss taken from the ceiling of one of the rooms in the old pub. This is carved with a boar, a badge of the de Veres, the semi-regal earls of Essex. This is one indication the house was once in their possession. The emblem also occurs in the stonework of the cathedral. Perhaps it was when the de Veres parted with their town house that it was called the New Inn.

Another relic from the inn was a cut-out, life-size figure of a chambermaid. This went to the White Hart, but what happened to it later I cannot trace. Such dummy boards, otherwise known as fireside figures, originated in Holland and were once quite common. Their purpose remains ambiguous. Stood before empty grates or in corners and in passages, they must have given a sense of occupancy in a rambling house. The Black Boy had two more – grenadiers painted by a local man. Initially, they flanked the entrance, and then they were moved to the stable yard. There was also a cockpit here, as at the Saracen.

Among the many visitors of note who put up at the Black Boy was Cosimo de Medici, Grand Duke of Tuscany. That was in 1669. William V of Orange stayed one night while he was taking refuge in Britain. In 1715, fifteen gentlemen, under suspicion of being Jacobites, were confined in the house. They did very well in their enforced leisure. Friends provided a handsome largesse. Among the many items on their bill of fare were twenty-two turkeys, nineteen geese, twenty-eight hares and 150 head of game and poultry. Their beverages were also prodigious. Well, they were kept here for nigh on three months.

The original hostelry went in 1854, not able to compete, it seems, with the railway, which had come to the town just a few years before. There was a short-lived successor on part of the site, but later Barnard's Temperance Hotel arose, the proprietor also in trade as a cabinetmaker. The corner is now occupied by a Martins, one of the newsagent chain.

A few yards away, by the bridge in Moulsham Street, there was the Cock Inn. According to title deeds, its original name was 'The Cocke and Coach'. Very old, it had leaded windows, an oak-panelled hall and a vast cellarage beneath. It has a mention in Foxe's *Book of Martyrs*, when Richard Potto was the innkeeper. Potto had taunted the Protestant George 'Trudge-over-the-World' Eagles on his way to execution. But Foxe, no doubt with some relish, recorded Potto's own end in 1559. Suddenly taken ill and helped to his bed by a servant, he 'fell like a lump of lead and, foaming at the mouth, never spoke afterwards'. He died several days later.

In 1898 the place of the Cock was taken by a huge Methodist church, which in turn came down in 1971 and is now Cater House, occupied by Presto's, the supermarket, and offices. Further along you could once have seen the Cross Keys. This became yet another victim of development. I could go on and on listing others. In 1916 the Regent Cinema was erected here. Recognizable from its façade, it now serves the devotees of Bingo. 'Time, gentlemen, please,' became 'Eyes down for a full house.'

There are many pub names which commemorate prestigious Essex families and personalities. At Maldon there is a hint of the de Veres again, for the Blue Boar Inn could have derived the sign from them. It is thought that one of the last earl's retainers may have been given the house. The old Falcon near the fortress at Castle Hedingham may be so called from the insignia of Sir John Hawkwood of Sible Hedingham. The fine timbered house has survived, but as a private residence. Briefly going back to Great Baddow, the sign of the Blue Lion here is from the arms of the Mildmays which had three lions rampant azure. This many-branched family held much land in and around Chelmsford, as well as elsewhere in Essex, for four centuries. At Herongate, Horndon, the picturesque Boar's Head with its duckpond takes the sign of the Tyrell family, 'a boar's head, couped and erect, argent, issuent out of the mouth a peacock's tail proper'. Their seat was Heron Hall, pulled down many years ago.

The extremely elegant Tower Arms, built in the Queen

Anne style in 1704 and standing opposite the church at South Weald, bears the name of the gentry at Weald Hall. They were there for just over 200 years, until the sale of the estate in 1946. It has become a lovely country park. Rivenhall and the neighbouring parish of Great Braxted both have pubs with local, ancestral names. At the former there is the Western Arms, which acquired the name while the Westerns were still lords of the manor. The Du Cane Arms at Braxted is from the family of merchants of Huguenot descent who traded with Italy and Russia. They bought the Park in 1751. The pub, spacious and plain, is well away in the village and is on the site of an alehouse which had the same name.

The Rayleigh Arms at Terling is known to locals as 'The Monkey'. This animal is one of the two supporters in the coat of arms of Lord Rayleigh of Terling Place, the other being a reindeer. This represents the Fitzgerald monkey, the very first Lady Rayleigh being a member of that family. The tradition is that when their Irish home caught fire in the fifteenth century, a pet monkey saved the infant heir by taking the child to the roof and then bringing him down to safety.

The names of several pubs testify to that fabled scourge of the road, the highwayman. The most notorious is said to have hidden in the excavation at Turpin's Cave, a pub at High Beech. Less well known, perhaps, is the Sixteen-String Jack in Theydon Bois. Jack Rann flamboyantly sported that number of silk strings on his breeches. He was executed in 1774.

While touching on criminal disorder, the George at Mountnessing, which I take to be the George and Dragon there now, was the scene of a dramatic arrest of smugglers. *The Chelmsford Chronicle* for 14 October 1774 reported it as follows: 'For some time past a gang of smugglers have been observed to frequent a public house at Mountnessing, and on Wednesday about five o'clock in the afternoon, two post-chaises full of custom-house officers, and their assistants, stopped at the George at that place; on their alighting they went into the house and seized two smugglers, who refusing to submit, several shots were engaged, one man was slightly wounded in the head, a smuggler received a shot in the leg, which shattered the bone in a terrible manner, and the ball lodged in his ankle. The officers afterwards made a very large seizure of teas, and lace which were concealed in hay-lofts and out-houses of that place, to the amount 'tis said of above 1000£.'

There are pubs with names of military distinction. Two can be found at Little Baddow. The Rodney is set well back on a hillside road and has many a nautical memento. Admiral Rodney's greatest victory was over the French fleet off Dominica in 1782. He was not an Essex man, but the link is with Captain Barrington who lived at 'Tofts' and who served under him. Closer in to the village centre lies the General's Arms, alluding to Major-General W.G. Strutt, brother of the first Lord Rayleigh. Much wounded in the service of his country, including the loss of a leg, he became a Governor of Quebec. He died in 1848. He, too, lived at Tofts. Before the pub took his name, it was the Warren.

The Sun, a simple, homely, if careworn house at Salcott-cum-Virley, figures in the pages of Baring-Gould's marshland novel *Mehalah* (1880). It is in a good position if you want, after due refreshment, to head on further to rinse your lungs along the saltings. In *Mehalah* it is given its older name, the Rising Sun. In striking contrast to how it looks today, the Rev. Baring-Gould described it as 'a low tavern ... a mass of gables; part of it, the tavern drinking room, is only one storey high, but the rest is a jungle of roofs and lean-to buildings, chimneys, and ovens, a miracle of pic-turesqueness'.

Of pubs with coastal and maritime associations, the Peter Boat on the front at Leigh-on-Sea has one of the most unusual names. It dates from the seventeenth century but with a restaurant has very much changed, the original house having been ravaged by fire in 1892. A Peter boat was a type of fishing vessel much used off the Essex coast from as early as 1580. They were made to sail either way, the stem and stern being alike. They took the name from Petermen, a term once used for fishermen, and obviously so called after St Peter who gave up his nets to become one of Christ's 'fishers of men'.

The Barge Inn at Battlesbridge is a reminder of the bygone activity on the Crouch. Another barge, the one at Vange, saw many a river sailor in the past when Timberlog Lane was used to transport wood to Vange Wharf, *en route* by water to London. Well over a century ago the Barge had a very curious name, 'The Man With Seven Wives'; the publican's name was Wife, and presumably seven was the number in his family. A Thameside pub at Tilbury, the World's End, was formerly a ferry-house for the crossing to Gravesend.

On Canvey, the King Canute has an engaging dual sign. It was the Red Cow but was renamed after the great inundation of 1953. A plaque in the saloon bar records that dramatic time. The primordial Flood in Genesis may have led to a Kelvedon alehouse being called the Noah's Ark. It went from the scene around 1860. But perhaps the sign came from the Shipwrights Company, whose crest had an ark and a dove with an olive branch in its beak.

So many pub names celebrate great naval figures, vessels and events in the remoter past that it is good to find at least one of our own age. This is the Matapan at Becontree, Dagenham. Built after the Second World War, it perpetuates the memory of the air-sea battle in 1941 when five Italian warships were sunk off Cape Matapan by British aircraft.

If we set aside the numerous pubs across the county with the fox, the hare and the hounds in their signs, there are still many closely allied with the hunt and the forest. There are a cluster where we would most expect them to be, in the area which has substantial remains of the most ancient woodlands. The Bald Faced Stag at Buckhurst Hill was marked as the Bald Stag on a map of 1768. It was from here that the colourful Essex Hunt set out every Easter Monday. Antony Trollope would certainly have known it when he hunted in these parts, starting from the Kennels in Old Harlow. The Reindeer, not the present one with that name, was a notable inn. Now as 'the Warren', it is the home of the Superintendent of Epping Forest. Two others at Buckhurst Hill are the Warren Wood House and the Roebuck Hotel, a Trusthouse Forte.

Epping itself has a Forest Gate, while not so far off at Hatfield Heath, near the Forest maintained by the National

Trust, there is the seventeenth-century Stag. Potter Street, lost in the post-war growth of Harlow, has a pub of the same age, the Horns and Horseshoes, although this may represent a coaching house. Harlow New Town must be mentioned here for the number of modern pubs with names of lepidoptera: the Drinking Moth, Essex Skipper, Purple Emperor, Small Copper, White Admiral and Painted Lady.

There are some pubs with ecclesiastical connections which have intrigued me. The Angel on the High Street in Kelvedon, now a large disco pub, could have taken its name like other Angels from a pre-Reformation sign depicting the Annunciation, the figure of the Virgin later being dropped. William III stopped off here in October 1692, travelling either to or from Holland via Harwich. The row of ancient houses which make up Knight Templars Terrace once formed an inn, the Red Lion. There is today a Red House in Church Street.

Church House in Romford, erected as the chantry for the parish church of St Edward the Confessor, became at the Reformation the Cock and Bell. It was returned to the church in 1908. At least it escaped the fate of an old chapel in Coggeshall. This was built in the sixteenth century, the money being bequeathed by a Thomas Hall in his will. Demolished in 1795, the Chapel Hotel stands on the site in Church Street.

A favourite halt of mine is St Anne's Castle at Great Leighs. It stands like a guardian on the main thoroughfare, at the Wantz corner on the A130. Its boast is to be the oldest licensed public house in England, and how I wish that claim could be substantiated, for it stands in the ranks of others which boldly assert this, including the Fighting Cocks in Abbey Mill Lane, St Albans.

Reginald Beckett came here around 1900, as he tells us in his *Romantic Essex*. He found it 'rather large for a roadside inn' and the sign then was written 'St Anna's Castle'. He was not too taken when he entered. 'It is very bare and forlorn within, and my tea was roughly though very civilly served.' It stays plain yet sturdy and has a decided air of former days. A haunting several years back 'made the papers' which has added to its attraction.

The house is on or very near the ground of a hermitage. Ogilby mentioned it as far back as 1675, and it is probably that alluded to by Taylor in 1636 when he wrote of a keeper of 'innes at Plashie [Pleshey] and St Anne's'. The 'Castle' was a later addition. Known as such by 1805, it may have come about from the appearance of the hermitage ruins or perhaps suggested by those of Leighs Priory. White tells us that the hermitage was a pilgrim hospice which at the Dissolution of the monastic houses went to a Thomas Jennings. This much, then, is true, that the spot, with perhaps a short interruption, has served the passing traveller from time immemorial.

I am almost at the end of this miniature survey, but there are two more curious signs to ponder on, one past and one present.

At Widford there was until this century a public house called the Silent Woman where a truly unusual pictorial sign was exhibited outside. One side of the board had a half-length portrait of Henry VIII. The other showed a headless woman dressed in a costume of old. Above her an inscription read *'Fort Bon'*, an untutored version of the French for 'Very Good'. It was popularly supposed she represented Anne Boleyn, but the sign as the Good Woman and the Quiet Woman is known elsewhere in the country, a good woman for many henpecked husbands being synonymous with a silent woman. Decapitation was the surest cure! It has been suggested that the two-fold image at Widford could have perpetuated a previous name for the tavern, the King's Head.

If you go to Woodham Walter and take the lane to Curling Tye Green, you will shortly come upon a lone house on the left. This is the Cats. It has a signboard which displays them, but up on an overhanging roof you will see a white and sculptured cat fixed to the tiles. On one of my visits to this pleasant house I asked at the bar if the pub had always had the name. 'Well,' said my informant after some deliberation, 'I have heard it was once the Scraggy Lion.' The look on his face, however, did nothing to induce conviction. Oddly, there is a companion piece for the crouching cat above a cottage door in the village. Somewhere behind these figures a tale waits to be pried out.

Do go there. The place has three pubs of varied character to choose from. And when you make the journey to these or any others, be it a Jerry house, a picturesque tavern or wine-bar, remember the warning lines of GKC in *The Flying Inn*:

> If an angel out of heaven
> Brings you other things to drink,
> Thank him for his kind intention,
> Go and pour it down the sink.

15

Cold Norton

At a first glance, Cold Norton with its beguiling name looks unpromising to the enthusiast for local colour and history. There is little by way of antiquity to be seen. It seems, in passing through, decidedly a suburban ribbon. Perhaps this is why it gets but scant notice in books on the county, the Three Rivers golf course being the major feature to get attention. Yet just a few hours of close research and sauntering around will show that the apparent lack of interest is misleading. Cold Norton's rural way of life has certainly been diminished, but only in the last few decades. It has only just become commuter country. Moreover, the past here has had its quota of outstanding names, and one at least in the present, that of Christina Foyle, who has a house on the fringe of the village. Nor is the landscape without attraction, if you know which path to take. It is time for justice to be done to the merits of this unassuming place.

The first recorded appearance of Cold Norton is in the Domesday Book, where it is entered simply as 'Nortuna', North Tun (village), most probably because of its location north of the River Crouch. Before the Conquest, the land was held by a freeman, one Wulfric. The Great Survey tells us its Norman overlord was Ralph Baynard, who held twenty-five manors in Essex from the Crown. (His name survives in the Baynard Castle Tavern on the corner of Queen Victoria Street in London.) All were seized when his grandson William was involved in a plot against Henry I, but they were restored to the family by Henry III, along with the privilege of hunting in all the king's forests in England, always a sure mark of royal favour.

St Stephen's, Cold Norton

In an Assize Roll of 1285 at the Public Records Office, Norton is called 'Norton juxta ffanbrigge', Norton near Fambridge. By 1350 we find the parish being styled by its present name. Oddly, in a document of 1605 it was written 'Coldnorton alias Gold Norton' but this seems an isolated instance of calling it such.

On Robert Morden's map of Essex (1695) it is shown as Norton Cold, as it is on that of Chapman & André in 1777. It is generally thought that the addition of Cold came about because of the exposed position of the land here. It also served to distinguish it from the other Norton in the county, little Norton Mandeville near Ongar. It was well named, especially in view of an entry in the parish registers in 1638, which recorded a frost of such severity that the Crouch froze over and people crossed by foot at Fambridge Ferry.

The village at its centre on Beacon Hill is less than three miles from the river, and the land here rises sharply to 156 feet above sea-level. This is in contrast to nearby North Fambridge, twenty-four feet at its highest point. To the west of the village at Great Canney, the elevation is 200 feet.

Morant's account of the parish gives the two ancient manors as that of Cold Norton Hall and that of West Whetenham and Flambards. The latter was at first part of the Hall lands and possibly developed from the lesser of Ralph Baynard's two holdings.

Cold Norton Hall had a number of notable owners down the years. It was successively part of the estates of the Fitzwalters of Woodham; of the mighty Bohuns, earls of Hereford and Essex; of the Staffords and the Bourchier family; and then passed via the Crown to Robert, Earl of Sussex. If they had any personal, domestic links with the Hall, they remain unknown.

In 1598 the Earl of Sussex conveyed the manor to Thomas Sutton, Esquire, when a William Walker resided here as the leaseholder. It was then of considerable substance. Apart from the manor house itself, it consisted of sixteen dwellings, two mills, one dovehouse, sixteen gardens, sixteen orchards, 600 acres of arable land, forty of meadow, 200 of pasture, twenty acres of woodland, forty of furze and heath, forty of marshland, free warren – namely, the right to game or rabbits – and fishing rights.

With Thomas Sutton we have a figure who is more than a mere name. He was one of the celebrities of his time, reputed to have been the richest commoner in England. A Lincolnshire businessman, he made his fortune in the coalfields of Durham after having been a soldier, and was for a time Master of the Ordnance in the North. He came to London in 1580. He founded the famous Charterhouse School in 1610, having bought the site for £13,000, although his death at seventy-nine the following year denied to him his ambition to be its first Master. His estate at Cold Norton was part of the endowment.

John Aubrey, as usual, provides us with some scurrilous entertainment about him. (I am sure that today Aubrey would be writing for *Private Eye*). Sutton, he tells us, 'a lusty healthy handsome fellow', married 'a young buxom widow' of a wealthy, aged brewer. She had 'enjoyed the embraces of this more able performer .... He was much upon mortgages and fed several with hopes of being his (the brewer's) heir.' Aubrey also tells us that towards the end of his life Sutton lived at a shop in Fleet Street 'where he had so many great chests full of money that his chamber was ready to groan under it'. It is a pity we have no facts, or even Aubrey-type hearsay, of his connections with Cold Norton. That he was sometimes at the Hall there can be no doubt.

The Governors of Charterhouse retain the lordship of Cold Norton Manor, and with the Lord Chancellor hold the advowson to the church – that is, the right to appoint the incumbent.

The second of the manors in the parish was smaller and of lower value. Yet this, too, has not been without prestige. The name of Whetenham seems to have fallen into disuse at an early date, while 'ham' suggests a lost settlement.

The first mention of the lovely-sounding Flambards comes in records of 1486, although it has been associated with a Joan Flambard of 1327, her name having been found in Subsidy Rolls at the PRO. Now a farm, Flambards has for some years been called Flambirds and is marked as such on the Ordnance Survey map. No doubt this has arisen from its old spelling as 'Flamberdes'. In recent years it has given its name to a popular novel and a television series. The book, by Anne Peyton, had for its setting the old airfield now under the plough. Among the manor's owners of old was the eminent Browne family. Sir John Browne, who hailed from Rutland, was Lord Mayor of London in 1480. His son by his second wife, Sir William Browne, also became the Lord Mayor in 1513. He died the following year. Both father and son were of the Mercers Company. In fact, William appears to have held the great office twice, for Stowe in his *Survey of London* also gives a William Browne, mercer, as Lord Mayor for part of 1507.

Sir William Browne's heir, also a William, married the daughter of yet another Lord Mayor of London, Ralph Dormer or Dodmer, who held the position in 1529. Later members of the Browne family also married well. Arthur Browne, living in 1664, was wed to the daughter of John Elmer of Mugdon Hall at Ulting. The Elmers there, several of whom were christened John, were descended from the John Elmer who had been Bishop of London until his demise in 1594. One of the Johns married Priscilla Clovile, daughter of Sir Henry Clovile of West Hanningfield.

Ownership of an estate does not, of course, necessarily imply habitual residence. Many properties were leased out or had a bailiff. But we know from the will of Thomas Browne that he lived at Flambards, his country house, and asked to be buried in the parish church. He was born in 1526; his will is dated 2 May 1567 and was proved a few days later. Although he was only forty-one, the will names four sons and two daughters. He must have lived at Flambards well, for he also had ten menservants. His wife was pregnant at the time of his decease. Morant does not give the ownership of Flambards in his day, but another source shows it then to have been a farm in the hands of a family called Clarke.

The long line of noblemen and gentry has quite gone, effaced by social changes, and so too has the church they knew. The church here now, dedicated to St Stephen, stands on the foundations of the medieval one. The ancient church was very small, having a twelfth-century nave and a wooden belfry with a short spire. The present building, of stone in the Decorated style, was erected in 1855 by the then rector and rural dean, the Rev. William Holland MA, at his own expense. It is 'all of a piece', made up of a nave, chancel and southern porch. Until a few years back there was a western bellcote which in Pevsner's judgement was 'quite out of keeping with the style of this part of Essex'. On the hill, it offers sweeping views which fall away to the south.

Most Victorian churches and restorations are not to my liking. I find them stuffy and sedate, designed for complacent landlords, lacking the grace and delicacy of the Gothic they so often in laborious fashion try to imitate. They are rather too self-important, driving out the spirit. But not so here. St Stephen's has an unobtrusive dignity in its open setting. It has no bourgeois smugness. Within its walls I have no feeling of an alien era, no severance from a vibrating past. Nor is that my feeling in the airy, cared-for churchyard. You must come here to sense just what I mean. It is one of those which speak with the words of E.E. Cummings:

i am a little church (no great cathedral)
... at peace with nature.

Inside, there are one or two items of antiquarian note, relics from the old derelict church. There is a brass of around 1520 showing the figure of an un-named woman. It has been dated from her type of head-dress. The oak reading-desk was carved from one of the original beams. In the churchyard stands a tombstone to William Walker JP who died in 1708. He was the father of sixteen children. I should think he was a descendant of the William Walker at the Hall in the reign of Elizabeth. His will of 1593 survives, along with that of his son.

This William Walker was accused in 1583 of allowing his house to be used for 'unlawful reading and catechizing'. This sounds like a conventicle, the term in use then for clandestine religious meetings not authorized by the Church. They were in effect cells for the growing Puritan dissent in the later years of Elizabeth's reign. When the great trial of strength with the Crown began in the next century, Essex was a hotbed of 'the godly' and sided in the main with Parliament.

Walker was soon in trouble again, in the very next year, when he was charged with going to communion in Maldon and not to his own parish church. The vicar in Maldon, also the town preacher, was Mr Gifford, zealous and unorthodox. Woe betide the sinner in those days. In the year in which Walker first became suspect, another parishioner was accused of immorality with his servant. He was called to repent publicly and to amend his life. In addition, he was ordered to present a copy of the revered *Book of Martyrs* to the church, and to give 20 shillings for poor scholars.

When the Presbyterians finally gained the upper hand in Parliament, the minister at Cold Norton, William Middleton, was deprived of his living. A safe man was put in in 1647. He was followed by other approved incumbents, and then Mr Thomas Hubbard. With the return of the monarchy it was his turn to be ejected, dying four years after.

In the church there is also a brass to Maude Cammocke, who died in 1599, the 'comfortable' wife of Robert

Cammocke, gentleman, of Layer Marney.

The old registers of the parish, with transcripts of them, are lodged now at the Essex Record Office. They date from 1539, which makes the series of particular value as the earliest year for the keeping of registers was 1538. They passed for a while into private hands, being sold in 1815 as part of the dead incumbent's effects, but they were subsequently re-purchased.

The social life of this village, as everywhere else, centred not only on the church but on the alehouse. Of the two pubs, the Norton, and the Stow Bullocks on the boundary with Stow Maries, it is the latter which has the greater ancestry. The forerunner of the present house was called the Fly and Bullock, more correctly listed by White in his *Directory* as the Flying Bullock. The sign was that of the Company of Butchers, from the winged ox of St Luke, their patron saint.

White gives us a glimpse into the structure of village life as it was in the middle of the last century. The Rev. W. Holland had 'a large and handsome residence' with forty-two acres of glebe land. Cold Norton Hall is described as 'a neat mansion, commanding extensive views'. With the farm, it was occupied by the Clarke family who had been there for over a hundred years. White lists a number of farmers but named only two farms, the Hall and Wild Farm. The National School had a house attached for the one and only mistress. The school was then new, having gone up in 1842. There was a shoemaker and a shopkeeper, with the Bullock being kept by Abraham Gabriel Taylor. The parish had only one ancient charity: the rent of a cottage, garden and just over an acre of land being given to the poor by an unknown donor. Let for £5, the income was added to the poor rate.

It is a striking contrast to turn from White's account to another nearly a hundred years later, namely that in *Kelly's Directory of Essex*, where Cold Norton is entered as 'a picturesque village'. In the list of addresses, private and commercial, what is particularly noticeable is the number of properties with names which reflect the elevation of the land e.g. The Rise, Hillside, Mount View, Hillsborough and Grand View. A total of fifteen farms is given, including six devoted to poultry. Eleven of those were smaller than 150 acres. Among the farms named are Flambirds, Blue House, Little Cooks, Way-Back, Little Canney and Wild Farm. A fruiterer had Purleigh View, a builder was at Moonrakers, and there were three shops, two of them on Beacon Hill. 'Tamina' was occupied by a coal merchant. A doctor's surgery was open once a week, run from Maldon Hospital. There is no doctor in the village now.

Apart from the Bullocks Inn, with its postal address given as Stow Maries, there was the Railway Hotel which has since become the Norton. The station, no longer here, was on the Maldon branch of the London & North-Eastern Railway. The track has also gone, leaving the bridge, with others along the route, as the only visible reminder of the line. There was a bus service daily to Maldon, Colchester and Southend. The village had a garage and a firm of agricultural engineers. The nearest post office was downhill in Stow Maries. Apparently, there were only several properties on the phone.

Such, then, are the vestiges of Cold Norton's placid history. No longer the insular place it was and although now growing apace, the parish has always had a very small population. Before the introduction of the national census, the number of parochial residents was often estimated by local clergy on the basis of 'houses' and 'families'. For Cold Norton nineteen or twenty families were given for 1723. In 1801 the return was twenty-four houses and forty-two families. The population remained very stable. In 1821 the census showed 226. Ten years on, it had gone down slightly to 216, while by 1848 it stood at 264. *Kelly* in 1933 recorded 384 for the civil parish. The census for 1971 gave a figure of 653, an increase of only 400-odd in 150 years!

No doubt the population will expand at a much-accelerated rate in the next few years, with the development of nearby Woodham Ferrers and its inevitable pull upon the remoter parts of the old Dengie hundred.

16

Ancestral 'Langleys' and Pleshey

You could hardly experience a sharper contrast between villages than to make a sudden transition from modest Cold Norton to the twin places which are the setting for this chapter.

Throughout Essex there are many landscape reminders of the old estates whose role was paramount in shaping the countryside and the pattern of rural life. Their decline was rapid from the time of the Great War, burdened with high costs and taxation, and when so many officer-sons of the gentry had fallen in battle, to lie in

> ... some corner of a foreign field
> That is for ever England.

Most of the manors, as such, have broken up, gone under the plough or the serried ranks of modern housing. Lordships remain, but they are for the most part nominal, mere privileges on parchment. The very expression 'estate' is now more applicable to the enclaves of Council dwellings or private speculators, while 'industrial estates' are legion. Yet here and there a landed property has survived with a family well rooted in the past. And not the least of these, of rare excellence, is 'Langleys'.

Heading north, the journey out from Chelmsford on the A130 is at first tedious and dull. The village of Broomfield is the final outpost of the county town before you get a glimmer of greener parts. But here the long tentacle of development halts. A little further on, the road, which forks to the left, takes you in moments to a different world: Great Waltham. Passing the Windmill on the left, a conspicuous

The south lodge at 'Langleys', Great Waltham

pub with a restaurant, and then a free house on the other side, you are quickly in the village. But just before reaching it there is Langleys, the mansion up in the parkland on the right, with a splendid gatehouse by the drive. Further along the highway, the fenced estate meets with the church, St Mary and St Lawrence. With the so-called guildhall, this corner on a bend – the first of two, the second dangerously sharp – is one of those sudden, visual surprises which will be long remembered by the most casual of travellers.

The parish is notable in more than one respect. With over eighty ancient buildings listed by the Royal Commission, it is enormous, the second largest in the county, the other being Writtle. Covering well over 7,000 acres, it stretches $5\frac{1}{2}$ miles from north to south. So great was the walking distance that for those who could not make it to the church a chapel of ease was erected at North End – the Black Chapel, which continues to stand, well preserved, at its lonely spot by the wayside.

Langleys is a massive red-brick house which stands on the foundations of a previous dwelling. The name, meaning 'long lea', has been traced back to 1280. Early in the Middle Ages it was also known as 'Marshalls'. Its history in those times is fragmentary and obscure. The long chronicle of the house really begins to come to life in the year 1515 with Thomas Everard.

The Everards were the first of the two distinguished families who have resided here. Thomas acquired one half of the manor. It was his heir, Richard, who by conveyance obtained the rest of the estate a few years later. When he died, in 1561, he held land not only in Great Waltham but in Felsted, Rayne, Little Dunmow and the Easters.

His successors fared very well. Antony Everard was one of many in the county to be knighted in 1603, the year of King James I's accession. Hugh Everard, who died in 1637, was a High Sheriff of Essex. His son, Sir Richard, became the first baronet of the family at the hands of Charles I. Of his two girls, one never married; the other, Elizabeth, wed Henry Osborne MA, vicar of Great Waltham, rector of West Hanningfield from 1713 for over twenty years, and finally vicar of Thaxted. He died in 1735 and from 1720 seems to have held the last two livings concurrently.

To return to Sir Richard, the baronet, in addition to his daughters he had three sons, each of whom made a name for himself, but two of them tragically. Moreton, the youngest, was killed while serving aboard the *Hampshire*, a vessel commanded by Lord Maynard of Easton Lodge. The second son, Hugh, perished on the Goodwin Sands. His brief, colourful sixteen years is recorded on his memorial in the church which I have quoted in Chapter 4. The third son, also with the Christian name of Richard, succeeded as the fourth baronet. He was to become a Governor of North Carolina. Heavily in debt, he and his mother, Dame Mary, were forced to sell Langleys in 1711. He bought a small estate in Broomfield. His wife, Susanna, was the daughter and heiress of Richard Kidder, Bishop of Bath and Wells, who was killed by falling chimneys in the memorable storm of 1703.

The family have other memorials in the parish church apart from that of the unfortunate Hugh. A brass of 1617 commemorates Richard and Clemence who were married for fifty-three years. The great attraction, however, is the alabaster and marble monument to Sir Antony Everard and to his first wife, Anne, related to Oliver Cromwell. She died in 1609. Dated 1611, the work has been beautifully restored, vivid in colour and gilding. In fact, Antony did not die until 1614, three years before his father depicted on the brass. The figures of the knight and his lady lie on two shelves within an arch, Anne's effigy above. Behind, two arched windows hold original stained glass. The couple had three children, and all died young: Richard and two who were lost as babes, unbaptized and perhaps stillborn. They are shown sculptured at the base of the wall-tomb, two little boys embracing, with the third child placed alone. The final touch of desolation is imparted with two small coffins.

I have come across a queer little tale from the days when the Everards lived in the old house. It first appeared in Beaumont's *Treatise of Spirits*. I know nothing of the author, although I wonder if he could be the Joseph Beaumont who lived from 1616 to 1699. (A poet, and a clergyman at Hadleigh, Suffolk, where he was born, he became a Professor of Divinity. He was also a Master of Jesus College and later Peterhouse. He was noted for an epic, *Psyche*, of 30,000 lines.) The story is on a par with much that characterizes the literature of 'true life' apparitions: anecdotal, and begging so many questions. But it makes good reading.

Sir Charles Lee, by his first lady, had only one daughter, of which she died in child-birth; and, when she was dead, her sister, the Lady Everard, desired to have the education of the child, and she was by her very well educated till she was marriageable, and a match was concluded for her with Sir William Perkins, but was then prevented in an extraordinary manner.

Upon a Thursday night, she, thinking she saw a light in her chamber after she was in bed, knocked for her maid, who presently came to her; and she asked, 'why she left a candle burning in her chamber?' The maid said she 'left none, and there was none but what she brought with her at that time'; then she said it was the fire, but that her maid told her was quite out; and said she believed it was only a dream, whereupon she said it might be so; and composed herself again to sleep.

But about two of the clock she was awakened again, and saw the apparition of a little woman between her curtain and her pillow, who told her she was her mother, that she was happy, and that by twelve of the clock that day she should be with her; whereupon she knocked again for her maid, called for her clothes, and when she was dressed, went into her closet, and came not out again till nine, and then brought out with her a letter sealed to her father; brought it to her aunt, the Lady Everard, told her what had happened and declared that as soon as she might be dead, it might be sent to him.

But the Lady thought that she was suddenly fallen mad, and thereupon sent presently away to Chelmsford for a physician and surgeon, who both came immediately; but the physician could discern no indication of what the lady had imagined, or of any indisposition of her body; notwithstanding the lady would needs have her let blood, which was done accordingly; and when the young woman had patiently let them do what they would with her, she desired that the chaplain might be called to read prayers; and when the prayers were ended she took her gittar and psalm-book, and sate down upon a chair without arms, and played and sung so melodiously and admirably, that her musick-master, who was then there, admired at it. And near the stroke of twelve, she rose and sate herself down in a great chaire with arms, and presently fetching a strong breathing or two, immediately expired, and was so suddenly cold as was much wondered at by the physician and surgeon.

She died at Waltham, in Essex, three miles from Chelmsford, and the letter was sent to Sir Charles at his house in Warwickshire, but he was so affected with the death of his daughter, that he came not till she was buried; but when he came he caused her to be taken up and to be buried with her mother at Edminton, as she desired in her letter. This was about the year 1662, or 63; and this relation the Lord Bishop of Gloucester had from Sir Charles himself.

When the Everards parted with Langleys in 1711, it was purchased by Samuel Tufnell, and so began the association with his family which has lasted to the present day.

Samuel Tufnell was twenty-nine when he took the house, and prominent in the City; his wife was the daughter of another London merchant, and she brought with her a dowry of £10,000. His great-grandfather, Richard Tufnell, had been a Master of the Salters Company, and on his death in 1636 had left 'an immense quantity of plate'. Richard's grandson married Elizabeth Jolliffe, and thus it was that the name came into the family and the Jolliffe crest to their coat of arms. Samuel was cultured and gifted. He wrote poetry, and antiquities became a life-long passion. A Fellow of the Society of Antiquaries, he took a particular interest in the past of Great Waltham, researched for him by the historian William Holman. He was an MP for Maldon and Colchester, and was sent on a diplomatic mission to Antwerp.

The Langleys we see today was his creation. He had the house refashioned (his was the general plan) but he kept several original rooms, encasing them in the north wing. The date of the newer house, 1719, is on a rainwater head. As it is never opened to the public, although at infrequent times the grounds and gardens are, some details on the structure and interior can meet our curiosity halfway.

Queen Ann in style, although a little later than her reign, it is 2½ storeys in height, with a frontage of 150 feet. There are a great many windows: fifty-six facing onto the park, thirty-six on the garden side. Imposing as it is on the elevated site, it is what lies inside that has aroused the greatest admiration, in particular the rooms of around 1620 which were preserved.

Two spacious rooms, one above the other, each measure thirty-six by twenty-two feet. The upper is the library, the lower the old dining-room. Of these Pevsner has said, they have 'plasterwork of an exuberance not exceeded anywhere in the county ... almost oppressively rich'. Both have highly ornamental fireplaces with allegorical figures, original with neo-Jacobean additions. One chimney-piece displays the central incident in the apocryphal story of Tobias. Pevsner's *Essex* in his *Buildings of England* series should be consulted for a closer description, and he provides a photograph as well.

When the first John Jolliffe Tufnell died, in 1792, his executors were at a loss to know what had become of the great sum of money he had realized shortly before. On searching in the library, a treasure was revealed behind the law books in the great bookcase. £150,000 and three caskets of jewels were brought to light. There was also a silver-gilt cup decorated with crystals, which was eventually sold in 1909 to the Goldsmiths Company for 5,000 guineas. This had come into the family through the marriage of Samuel Tufnell and Elizabeth Cressener and had been made for Sir John Cressener in 1503.

Of the several gatehouses on the perimeter of the grounds, the lodge at the entrance to the south drive is the most eye-catching. White, pedimented and emblazoned with a coat of arms, it bears the family motto in Latin: 'Being rather than seeming to be'. It is a miniature of the house itself. Behind, there is a wide and lengthy vista. The park, of a hundred acres and once stocked with deer, is superbly landscaped, the work of Charles Bridgeman, who has been credited with the invention of the ha-ha. Samuel Tufnell, in order to give himself a more commanding space in front of his mansion, obtained permission to divert the main Chelmsford to Dunmow road. Old oaks are a feature, and a great chestnut is of particular note. There is also a wild garden and walks which wind through the trees. A public footpath traverses part of the estate, a section of the Essex Way. This passes a cemetery for animals, crosses two little bridges (the stream is a tributary of the Chelmer) and goes on to Chatham Green.

As we should expect, the parish church has memorials to the family. There are hatchments in the nave. The reredos behind the altar was set up in 1894 in honour of Colonel A.J. Tufnell. Soldiers have figured prominently in the family.

Major William Tufnell was a Troop Commander of the Essex Yeomanry in the Napoleonic Wars.

Colonel Tufnell was succeeded by W.N. Tufnell. He, too, had the rank of colonel. Mentioned a number of times in the pages of the Rev. Clark's wartime diaries, he comes through as awkwardly independent. Not caring for the minister at Ford End, he attended church at Pleshey. He used to motor there, which led to his being summonsed for breaking the emergency regulations on petrol then in force.

The greater part of Pleshey was, and still is, the property of the Tufnells who hold the lordship. It is a most remarkable place. The parish is little over 700 acres in extent, one of the smallest in the county. It could with legitimate exaggeration be called the Avebury of Essex, for although it lacks the greater antiquity of the Wiltshire settlement and the monumental standing stones surrounding it, which are Avebury's magnetic attraction, Pleshey is comparable in having once been totally encircled by earthworks, their line well brought out by aerial photographs. It ranks as one of the great defensive sites of medieval England, a place of major civic and military importance in its heyday. To stand on the summit of the focal point, the fifty-foot-high mound, is to be at the hub of our baronial history.

The mount or *motte* lies south of the main village street, a Roman road. The manor, held in late Saxon times from the Abbots of Ely, was granted by the Conqueror to Eustace, Count of Boulogne. Later it was given by King Stephen to Geoffrey de Mandeville. He it was who began the first castle here, raising the mound to its present height, the top half being entirely artificial, and in doing so created the moat around it. The original Norman fort would have been a stout wooden tower surrounded by a stockade. At a later stage this was replaced by a stone keep which has quite gone. In front was the first or inner bailey, a vast courtyard filled with ancillary buildings, and this, too, had protective earthworks. There are so many undulations hereabouts that Leland tells us that Pleshey was once known to its inhabitants as 'Tumbletown'.

Although the layout in its completed form is difficult for the layman of today to visualize clearly, there is no such obstacle to the imagination in viewing the fine bridge which, with a single high arch, spans the moat, unique in Britain. It was cloaked in ivy not so many years ago; now we can see the structure in full, 'almost certainly the most ancient brick bridge in Europe'. At least fifteenth century in origin, it could be even older.

Having risked all in going over to the Empress Maud, Geoffrey de Mandeville was imprisoned in the Tower and his estates were seized. Henry II restored the lands to his son, the second Geoffrey, who continued his father's work at Pleshey. For well over two centuries the Lord High Constables of England made the castle their principal residence.

The outermost line of defence was the entrenchment which went right round the village. Today, this can be easily traced on foot as a series of conspicuous, deep ditches, in places emblazoned with primroses in the spring. It remains a possibility that this extensive system is pre-Roman in origin.

There are other things of historic interest here even though they have left no visible trace. But the most grievous loss was the College of Chaplains founded by Thomas of Woodstock, Duke of Gloucester, in 1393, four years before his tragic end. A short history of the college, and its modern counterpart, the Diocesan House of Retreat, can be found in Margaret Avery's book on Pleshey. I purchased my copy at the bar of the White Horse.

The collegiate church, dedicated to the Holy Trinity, witnessed some notable burials, among them the daughter of the founder and her grandson, Humphrey Stafford, Duke of Buckingham, who was slain at the Battle of Northampton in 1460. His son, Sir Henry, who married the mother of Henry VII, was also interred here. When in the reign of Edward VI the manor with its parks went to Sir John Gate, he proceeded to pull down the college buildings. (He was to pay the supreme penalty for supporting Lady Jane Grey.) The transepts and the chancel with its tombs were demolished, but the rest of the church was saved by being purchased by the parishioners. Most of this in turn went in 1708, to be replaced by a small brick church.

The story of the death of Thomas, Duke of Gloucester,

and the subsequent decline of the castle, is fairly well known, as are the references to Pleshey in Shakespeare. Having been cordially visited at the castle by his uncle, Richard II, Gloucester accompanied the King back to London, only to be suddenly arrested at Stratford by Bow. He was then spirited away to Calais. Officially he died there of apoplexy, but there is little doubt he was put to death, suffocated between two feather beds. Such is the account given by the contemporary Froissart. The Duke's body was embalmed and brought back to his church for burial, but it may later have been transferred to Westminster Abbey.

His wife, Eleanor, having retired to Barking Abbey, held the estate for two more years before she died. It passed through other hands, notably to Thomas, Lord Rich, and to Sir Robert Clarke. Then, in 1749, it was acquired by Samuel Tufnell on the death of his bachelor uncle, the eighty-five-year-old Sir William Joliffe.

It is due to the Tufnells that the village stays undisturbed, unspoilt and compact. They have preserved its identity. In the eighteenth century it was described as 'a set of miserable houses, or rather huts', and Coller, quoting this in 1861, added 'and not even yet much improved'. But that is not the picture today. A number of cottages have been saved from demolition as old-timers with little means have gone. In the main street, where there are houses backing onto the moat, I have witnessed the transformation of several into a single, picturesque home.

At the very western end, just beyond the White Horse, there stands the present church of the Holy Trinity. Rebuilt in 1868 by Chancellor, it is an appropriate spot at which to conclude a visit. It contains unfigured brasses and a stone inscribed '*Ricardus Rex II*' rescued from the past. Here, too, is the monument to Samuel Tufnell. It is a place in which to give thanks, as his present-day successor, the liberal patron of the clearance and excavations at the castle, continues the great tradition of the family in making the history of Langleys and of Pleshey a perennial stream.

17

'Mesopotamia' and Other Curiosities

I think it has to be admitted that, for visible evidence of the past, Chelmsford is disappointing. For period charm it must rank low in the league for county towns. Relentless commercial enterprise has for decades overlaid the past here, leaving but lone sentinels of how it appeared before the present century. Physical clues are sparse; for what has gone we must turn in the main to old books, prints and maps. The centre of Chelmsford today vies with that of Basildon as a mecca of stores and offices.

There can be few among the shoppers streaming through the town who are aware that only yards away behind the High Street there was the area formerly called 'Mesopotamia Island'. Backing onto the Chelmer, this was a space once completely open but now taken up by car-parks and recent buildings. A strange old custom was enacted here each year, a mock election which coincided with that for the county. The 'candidates' first paraded through the streets on horseback, each accompanied by a page. Those who were successful at the polls were then chaired shoulder high and finally ducked in the river. The concluding ceremony on this rumbustious day was the breaking of the chairs. 1830 was particularly noted 'for an unusual display of wit and oratory' when the contestants 'were not less objects of popular applause than the more learned gentlemen of whom they were typical'.

As the spot was subject to frequent inundation, being near the confluence of the Cam and the Chelmer, this would seem to account for its name – Mesopotamia (or to give it its modern name, Iraq) having been periodically flooded by the

The Ghastly Miller of Billericay

Tigris and the Euphrates. One would like to know the name of the wit who gave birth to the analogy.

Only yards away there is another place with watery associations. Conduit Street recalls the ancient water supply for the town. The conduit, surmounted by a dome and a gas lamp, was in 1814 erected opposite the Shire Hall, where water had gushed from a well for centuries. An inscription here read: 'This conduit in one minute runs one hogshead and a half, and four gallons and a half. In one day 2,262 hogsheads and 54 gallons. In one month, 63,000 hogsheads. And in one year, 825,942 hogsheads and 54 gallons.' (One hogshead equals fifty imperial gallons.) In 1842, when it had become solely ornamental, the conduit was removed to the junction between the High Street and Springfield Road. There it remained, an obstacle to the growing traffic, until as late as 1940. Although taken down, it has been preserved.

As the mind travels, it is a quantum leap from the crowded pavements of Chelmsford to the village of Rickling, tucked away on the far north-west of the county, close to the border with Hertfordshire.

I well remember the first time I went there. It being close on opening time, I gravitated to the Cricketers Arms. Although there are many pubs with the name, the one here, which faces an impressive green, is of rare interest, for it witnessed the most phenomenal score in the history of English cricket. A worn old graphic sign hangs outside, displaying the game as it used to be played, with curved bats.

There was only one other occupant in the bar at that early hour, an aged local in the corner. Striking up a conversation – inevitably with a prelude on the weather – I bought him a pint. Soon he fell silent and drew his privacy about him. Moments later, having pondered over his glass, he raised his eyes and said, slowly and with emphatic pleasure and no small wonderment, 'Yer know, each morning when I wakes up, I thinks to meself, Christ, I'm still alive!' There could be no comment on that. I was reminded of another countryman of happy memory, the late Dick Weston of Stock, who would so often greet you beaming with the words, 'Isn't it good to be alive!' Such men make their own sunshine in their final years.

An aged man [wrote Yeats] is but a paltry thing,
A tattered cloak upon a stick, unless
Soul clap its hands and sing, and louder sing
For every tatter in its mortal dress.

Contemporary details of the memorable two-day match played on the green in August 1882 can be seen framed in the saloon bar. The village team batted first and were all out for 94. Then the Orleans Club went in on the second day and scored 920 runs! In the bar, as well, you will find two cricket bats bearing many famous signatures, including those of Hutton, Hammond, Don Bradman and Compton.

There is another and quite bizarre oddity to be looked for here in Rickling. When I left the pub, I went to the church. In a dim corner I came upon this inscription, having brushed away the dust:

It was the deceased's advice
to the living that noe
man should suffer 110
ounces of blood to be taken from him.

The unfortunate victim of the grotesque 'remedy' of blood-letting, carried to what must have proved a deadly excess, was one Robert Horton, whose remains lie here with those of his wife. But perhaps that amazing '110' should read as '10' or even 'No'.

At the other end of the county there is another solitary church with a relic far from ecclesiastical which gives us a true tale of the unexpected. This is the church of St Nicholas at Little Wigborough. It stands on the edge of a farmyard at the far end of a no-through lane, looking out, some ten feet above sea-level, to the Salcott Channel, Old Hall Marshes and the broad estuary of the Blackwater. This is indeed a remote place, shared only by Copt Hall, small but appealing, and several cottages. It can hardly be styled a village. With the twin parish of Great Wigborough, the combined population is little more than 200.

The 'noiseless tenor of their Way' has only twice been violently disturbed, on both occasions by literally soil-shaking events.

The church was one of those in the region wrecked in the major earthquake of 1884. The rector, writing to the *Morning Post* after the trauma, told how the church had been 'perfectly riddled'. Nave and tower had been rent asunder, and the roof stripped of its tiles. At first it was thought that all was beyond repair, but a brass plate inscription commemorates the restoration of the church within two years of the 'quake. Apparently, this is the sole memorial to be found anywhere in Essex to this most surprising of events.

But the church is guardian to another unique memento. High on the tower, on the inside wall, there hangs a small section of an aluminium girder, all that remains of a second bolt from the blue which hit the parish in September 1916.

The night of the 23rd/24th was a sensational one in the history of Essex at war. A raiding zeppelin, the L32, was shot down by a plane over Billericay and fell in flames on Snails Farm. Its companion, the L33, was damaged by gunfire and at first made for the coast. In the early hours of the morning it passed over Mersea but, losing height, turned back. With its engines failing – sounding, as someone said, like the death rattle in the throat – the monstrous shape hovered low in the starry sky above the marshes, a sky so bright that the rector of Great Leighs, the Rev. Andrew Clark, noted in his diary that one could see a needle. Then the airship came down, ploughing across a field, and came to rest blocking the road at Little Wigborough. What happened then has elements of tragi-comedy.

The zeppelin, 750 feet in length, had narrowly missed two cottages. The twenty or so of its crew scrambled out, and its commander prepared to set it alight. But first the Germans tried to rouse the occupants of the houses, which were in darkness. Having assured themselves they were empty – the residents, however, were crouching under the stairs – the crew then fired the ship. As it blazed, they disarmed themselves and marched off in the direction of Colchester to find someone in authority to whom they could surrender. By a very odd coincidence, one of them had worked in the town before the war.

The marching column encountered a police sergeant, one

of the Specials, near Peldon. Another, not in uniform, joined them on the march. Soon a local JP and his wife, cycling to the scene of the descent, were in the unlikely procession. One man in the neighbourhood, who, although described as a cripple, was able to ride a motorbike, went on to alert the military stationed at the Strood, the crossing to Mersea. He collided with a car in the blackout, and it was said he later died in hospital of his injuries. By daylight, the Germans, having grudgingly accepted arrest by the Specials, were firmly in the hands of the Army. The airship after burning out was left a skeleton and with its engines largely intact.

There is a nice postscript to the story. I have read, though it is hard to credit, that not long after an infant was taken to the font at Little Wigborough and christened Zeppelina Clark! Small the parish may be, but it has certainly clung to the memories of these events which briefly put it on the national map.

Windmills are far from being curiosities, for those which are left, although bygones, stand in the landscape in a natural and familiar alliance with the sky. At one time in the last century there were 200 in Essex alone. Now there are barely twenty which we cherish. But there are strange tales to be found about millers, none more peculiar than that of the Ghastly Miller of Billericay.

The sources for the life of the miller Thomas Wood lie in rare volumes, the *Transactions of the College of Physicians* for 1771 and the second edition of Herbert Mayo's *The Philosophy of Living* (1838). In the first instance, the facts derived from the then vicar of Great Burstead, a churchwarden and Wood's apothecary.

Thomas Wood was born in 1719. He was a sickly boy and had smallpox at thirteen. However, in early manhood he was healthy enough and built the second of Billericay's mills. He soon acquired a reputation for his eating-habits and for corpulence. Until he was forty-three, he dined heavily three times a day on fat meat and consumed great quantities of strong ale. But he then began to suffer a whole catalogue of ills: gout, rheumatism, epileptic attacks, constant thirst and sensations of suffocation.

In 1764 he was lent a book by the rector of a nearby parish. This was *Discourses on a Sober and Temperate Life*, a very popular tract judging from the number of times it had been translated from the original Italian. On taking its prescriptions to heart, Wood began to reduce his intake. At first he cut his drinking to a pint a day and ate meat sparingly. Then he gave up beer altogether and drank only water. He had a cold bath twice a week (the *Transactions* noted, 'This now daily luxury was then a medical treatment only resorted to in severe cases') and he took regular exercise with dumb-bells. He frequently gave up drinking water for months and subsisted on pudding made from sea-biscuit and on dumplings. Whenever he made a journey of some hours from home, he carried flour in his pockets. It was estimated that through his diet and fasting he lost ten or eleven stone. The only drawing of him shows him as lean rather than emaciated, although he must at times have looked haggard enough to earn him the nickname of 'Ghastly'. He was able to hump two sacks of meal with ease.

Wood died aged sixty-three in 1783 and lies with other members of the family at Great Burstead. He was an engaging local figure in other ways. A successful bee-keeper, he was also a lover of flowers and of birds, quite tame in his garden. He also staged firework displays by his mill. With his departure, the town lost a colourful personality.

A miller of very different note was Isaac Mead. Should you go to Beauchamp Roding, make the wide sweep around St Botolph's, the isolated Church in the Fields, and continue on towards the hamlet of Birds Green; you will shortly come to the drive to Hornets Farm on the right. I went there on a bright November day, leaves crackling underfoot and the cold touching the bone. By the wayside, in an overgrown, secluded corner, is a tiny burial plot, a very private, consecrated place of rest. If you disturb the bushes, and I had to break the twigs to get through, you will see four leaning stone crosses which mark interments of the Mead family. In this desolate spot, a six-foot obelisk stands over the grave of Susan Mead, wife of Isaac. It bears these simple, much-worn words:

TO THE GLORY OF GOD
AND
IN MEMORY OF
AN
ESSEX LASSIE
1924
AND

The inscription was never completed. Instead, a marble slab beneath is a memorial to her husband who lived on until 1945. Their lives, now a largely forgotten rural epic, share in the near-oblivion of this garden tomb.

A year before Susan was laid here, at her own request, there was printed in Chelmsford a small volume called *The Life Story of an Essex Lad, Written by Himself*. This is the plain autobiography of Isaac Mead, one-time farmhand, master miller and finally tenant of Hornets Farm, which he rescued from dereliction. The foreword was written by the Rev. Edward Gepp of High Easter, a local historian who achieved particular distinction for his *Essex Dialect Dictionary*.

Isaac's book, with its home-spun philosophy, gives a vivid grass-roots picture of country living and agriculture before urban values transformed village life. It reads as a celebration of himself and of his parents, yet totally without bombast. With a quiet piety, he brings all the old virtues to the fore: integrity, honour, thrift, hard work, self-help and neighbourliness. In these he was nourished by his favourite authors, such moral giants as Bunyan, Defoe and Dickens. Hardly a national event figures in the pages; there is not a mention of the Great War and its impact. All is a tale of toil and 'getting on', of farms and mills, and the keeping of animals. It is served like a meal which comes straight from the garden to the kitchen.

Isaac Mead was born in 1859 at High Easter. As a boy, from the age of eleven, he tended sheep, and in gathering acorns he broke a leg, which laid him up for many months. He then went onto the land, cutting corn with a sickle and gaining experience in draining the fields. When he was fifteen he used a scythe for the first time and a year or so later was threshing with a flail. In 1876 he was taken on at High

Easter windmill. In the great gale on New Year's Day the following year he saved it from running out of control. From the weather-loop, he witnessed the fall of the postmill at White Roding. (It was rebuilt as a towermill and remains there today in private ownership.) In 1880 he went to work for W.H. Marriage & Sons, employed at Blasford Hill, between the villages of Broomfield and Little Waltham, and filled in as well as Croxton Mill nearby. But very shortly after he was at Springfield Mill as a working foreman.

January 1881 was memorable for a severe snowstorm on the 18th, 'Black Tuesday'. More importantly for Isaac Mead, this was the year in which he went into business for himself. He was able to raise a loan to acquire Waples Farm, along with its two mills, one of which was driven by water. The windmill was later badly damaged in a storm and in 1910 destroyed by an accidental fire. Isaac was to comment, ruefully, 'This blessed thing I had kept insured for twenty odd years, but for the last two years had omitted to do so.'

After being engaged for five years, he married Susan Jane Smith at High Easter Chapel in 1880. She gave him four sons.

His final move, for which he does not give the date, was to Hornets. It would seem that in his last years he relinquished the title, for in 1933 it was listed in the names of three of his sons. I have been told that one grand-daughter survives, living in Abbess Roding.

Today the farmhouse is in other hands. Until around 1970 a second and highly unusual reminder of Isaac Mead's presence could be found here. This was an old chapel window with leaded lights, rescued by Isaac from a breakers' yard at Tottenham Hale and then installed in the end wall of a barn. When the new owners came, taking a house and outbuildings in great decay, the barn with its lancets had gone beyond repair and had to come down.

Placing that window had been a deeply felt act of commemoration. It marked the last of Isaac Mead's good works brought to a successful conclusion. For years he had taken the lead in the campaign to bring about the de-rating of agricultural land in which he won the ear of Winston Churchill. In achieving his objective, Isaac won a brief and extra-parochial fame. Yet he is now but a footnote in the pages of our farming history. The eclipse of this man is made all the more telling by a few quiet minutes spent at this sequestered and forlorn corner on an Essex lane.

While on the subject of unlikely tombs, there is one in the parish church of St Peter's at Sible Hedingham which merits a visit. There is a twin-tale of mystery and martial fame to the place. This is seemingly no grave, however, for there is no certainty it ever held a corpse. It serves instead as a cenotaph. It commemorates Sir John Hawkwood, that soldier of fortune *extraordinaire*, and may well have been intended as his final resting-place.

Hawkwood was born in the parish around 1320. According to tradition, his father, Gilbert, was by occupation a tanner, and yet he held much property hereabouts and was the lord of two manors. As a youth, John was apprenticed to a tailor in the City. Then, according to one account, he was pressed into the army of Edward III. But another implied it was by choice: 'He threw away the needle for the sword and the thimble for the shield.' It was the early phase of the Hundred Years War, and he quickly rose to be a captain and was later knighted after serving with the Black Prince at Poitiers.

Once released from royal duty he embarked on his career as a mercenary, joining the adventurers known as 'the Late Comers' who scourged the eastern provinces of France even to the gates of Avignon, where they harried the Pope. His Holiness bought them off and pardoned their many offences.

John Hawkwood now took command of the celebrated and notorious White Company, a powerful marauding force of 5,000 horsemen and 1,500 foot soldiers. Taking his highly disciplined mercenaries into Italy, he served the rulers of Pisa, Padua, Milan and Florence, frequently changing sides in the veering balance of power between the city-states. Always with his eye on the highest bidder, he established himself as the leading figure among the *condottieri* of the age. To the Italians he was known as Giovanni Acuto. Several times he held ambassadorial rank, and he attained near-princely status by his marriage into the ruling Visconti family of Milan. This was his second marriage, and his wife bore him several children, one of whom, John, later came to England and was given a knighthood by Henry IV.

When Hawkwood died, in 1394, he was given a magnificent public funeral and interred in the cathedral at Florence. His monument there has a fresco by Paolo Uccello in which he is portrayed as a statuesque figure mounted on a horse.

What then of the tomb-chest in the south aisle of the Essex village church, such a world away from all this turbulence and splendour? Sir John had kept his links with his birthplace and estate, and is said to have given instructions for a tomb here. We know, too, that at the request of Richard III the republic of Florence granted Hawkwood's widow the right to transfer his remains to England. There is no evidence, however, that she chose to do so.

The 'sepulchre' is not what it was. Early in the eighteenth century there could still be seen paintings on the wall within the ogee arch, showing Sir John and his two wives standing devoutly, each with a prayer-scroll issuing from the mouth. The now blank shields were once emblazoned with the arms of his companions. Among the carved devices which decorate the monument is a hawk; there are others on the church tower.

It is an easy transition from these oddities of mortality to read of some of the more unusual items to be found in old wills; unusual, that is, to our generation. I must admit to deriving an enjoyment from reading wills, especially those as remote in time as the sixteenth and seventeenth centuries. This pleasure comes all the more readily when the decipherment of the handwriting and of archaic words has been done by others. Two collections of such wills have been published under the auspices of Essex County Council. These are volumes IV and V of Dr F.G. Emmison's series *Elizabethan Life*, a superlative compilation from original Essex documents of that age. They excel in giving a vivid, detailed panorama of family life and environment. Certainly, for me, many of the wills held by the Essex Record Office at Chelmsford reveal homes as clear and authentic as can be seen in paintings of Dutch interiors.

Legacies of money, coins and jewellery abound. Thus, we can read of 'angels', coins 'good and old, and of the old stamp', being half-sovereigns in value and engraved with the figure of St Michael the Archangel slaying the dragon. There were also 'royals' and 'nobles'. These latter were of superior gold, last minted in the reign of Henry VIII. Rings were frequently left to relatives and friends, including signet rings and others with a death's head, bestowed for particular remembrance. Some rings were engraved with words. In one will 'a small gold ring with Moses Tables in it' was left, a miniature Decalogue or Ten Commandments. In another, that of Sir Antony Brown of South Weald, money is stipulated for rings to be inscribed with a posy: 'Wee dye' to appear on one side, and 'Forgett nott' on the other.

Benjamin Gonson, who lived at Saybrightes or Seabrights in Great Baddow, bequeathed 'a piece of gold worth 50 ducats' to 'Sir John Hawkins knight for a remembrance of my good will'. It would need to be checked, but this would seem to indicate a friendship with the great sea-dog of that era. Gonson's will is dated 1594 but was not proved until six years later. Hawkins died in 1595, so if he is the knight mentioned, he would not have received the prized nugget.

Examples of such treasures could be cited almost *ad infinitum*. They are in stark contrast to the lack of what we regard as basic household comforts.

Of course, gifts of money, heirlooms and adornments figure largely in the wills of today. But an item in the lengthy testament of Lady Waldegrave would be hard to match now, telling us she was leaving 'my still waters and medicines belonging to surgery and physic'. A sign of the times left its mark on a will of 1603 from Hatfield Peverel, 13s.4d being left for the poor with the stern proviso 'requiring my executors that none suspected or detected in the devilish art of sorcery or witchcraft have any part'.

A few wills throw light upon the books read then, particularly on the libraries of the educated gentry. Sir Thomas Smith of Hill Hall at Theydon Mount was notable for his learning. (His mansion is now being restored after serving for some years as a women's prison.) In his will of 1576 he wrote: 'Because I see that none of those which shall succeed me of long time are learned I give my Latin and Greek books to the Queen's College in Cambridge, and my great globe of my own making, so the Master and Fellows, having warning so soon as I am dead or at the least so soon as I am buried or before, the which I would they should have with a true inventory carried to them of the said books, do send carts to fetch them away within 10 or 12 days, the which I give on condition that they chain them up in their library or distribute then amongst the Fellows such as will best occupy them.' He then proceeded to list several authors by name: Titus Livius, the Roman historian whose prose was particularly esteemed for its polished rhetoric; Tully, better known as Cicero, another classical arbiter of excellence; and 'Aristotle in Greek and Plato in Greek and Latin'.

We would expect to learn of such erudite texts in the household of one like Sir Thomas Smith. It is much more surprising to find their like in the will of John Bentley, 'servant to Sir John Peter of Ingatestone knight'. This servant was no menial, however. A.C. Edwards in his book *John Petre* (Regency Press, 1975) has brought him partially from the shadows. Bentley kept Sir John's accounts and held first place in the hierarchy of Lord Petre's employees on the estate. His will of 1596 shows us a cultivated man who lived in no small style, and it merits an extensive quote. To his son George he bequeathed

> ... my great ring of gold that I daily wear having seal of a maiden's head graven upon it, my great chest of wainscot which standeth in my chamber at Ingatestone, the chest with my evidences of West Horndon' – these evidences being estate papers – 'and my yeoman chest here; and all my sets of song books and songs in rolls and my books for the virginals, all the books he now hath in custody, and Cowper's Dictionary in the large volume, Barratt's Dictionary, a Thomasin's Dictionary, all my other dictionaries in Greek and Latin or other languages whatsoever, Tully's offices with Commentaries, all my books pertaining to divinity as well in English as in Latin, and all other my books in English written or printed whatsoever, with my statute books and law books, one pair of virginals, my maps and arms, 1 silver bowl, 2 silver spoons, my best gown and my best cloak.

He did not, of course, forget the master and mistress to whom he owed so much. To Sir John he gave 'my new bible in Latin in quarto of Venice print, imprinted in the year of our Lord God 1587, which I do beseech him to take as a small remembrance of me, not having anything better to bestow upon him'. For Lady Petre there was 'a very fruitful and pleasant book called the Instruction of a Christian Woman made by Ludovicus Vives, and 20s in gold'. John Bentley's love of music would certainly have been nourished by listening to the composer William Byrd, a frequent visitor to the Petres, his patrons, long before he made his home at Stondon Massey.

I end this random harvest of curiosities with a really singular will from the eighteenth century, printed in the *Essex Review* in 1910, remarkable and rare for its imprint of a forceful personality. It is the will of John Redman, dating from 1798, and although some words are missing, I give it here as entire as it has come down to us, for through it I fancy I can see an old man, fiercely independent, shaking his fist at death.

The last Will of John Redman, citizen of the world, of Tylehurst Lodge Farm, Upminster, in Essex .... My body to be buried in the ground in Bunhill Fields, where my grandfather, Captain John Redman, of the Navy, in the Queen Anne's reign, lies interred'. [This is an odd error, for the Captain lies at rest in the churchyard at Upminster. The will continues]: My grave to be ten feet deep. Neither gravestone, atchment, escutcheon, mutes, nor porters at the door, and to be performed at seven o'clock in the morning ... all my wine to be drunk on the premises, or to be shared by, and between my four executors .... Tilehurst Lodge Farm I devise to the eldest son of my second cousin, Mr Benjamin Branfill, on condition that he, the eldest son, takes the name of Redman, or to his second or the third son, if the others decline it. It is hereby enjoined to the Bramfills to keep the owner's apartment and land in hand, to be a check on shuffling, sharping tenants, who are much disposed to impoverish the land.

Having provided handsomely for my daughter, Mary Smith Ord, on her marriage with Craven Ord, of the Cursetors Office, London, I hereby bequeath to her children born, or to be born (the eldest son excepted, whose father will provide for him) the sum of two thousand pounds to each of them at the age of one and twenty, for which I bequeath all my valuable estates at Greensted, and Ongar, late Robotiers .... Holding my executors in such esteem, I desire them to pay all the legacies without the wicked swindling and base imposition of stamps, that smell of blood and carnage .... To Mr French, of Harpur Street, a set of Tom Paines, Rights of Man, bound with common sense, with the answers intended by the longheads of the law, fatheads of the church, and wiseheads of an insolent usurping aristocracy .... To that valuable friend of this country in the worst of times, Charles Fox, member for Westminster, five hundred guineas. To each of the daughters of Horne Tooke, five hundred pounds.

There is a codicil to the will, but before giving this as the final flourish, there are one or two points in the text which call for some explanation.

The hatchment, or 'atchment' as Redman puts it, was the large board painted with the armorial bearings of the deceased. Frequently of lozenge shape, they were part of the funeral trappings, affixed to the house and later placed on the walls of the parish church. Many can still be found *in situ*. 'Mutes' were hired mourners.

The Rev. Craven Ord, who lived at Greensted Hall beside the Saxon church near Ongar, was an antiquarian, especially noted for his brass rubbings. He died in 1832 and lies in the churchyard of St Andrew's. He had been a cursitor, a Chancery clerk. As for the reference in the will to the Hall as 'late Robotiers', Morant noted in 1768, 'It belongs now to David Rebotier Esq.'

John Horne Tooke (1736-1812) was a turbulent character. While at school he had lost the sight of his right eye in a brawl. A philologist and a radical politician, 'the philosopher of Wimbledon', he was a friend of Wilkes until they quarrelled. But despite the effectiveness of his pen he made little impression on the House of Commons as Member for the rotten borough of Old Sarum.

The great freethinker Thomas Paine and his book *The Rights of Man* should be familiar to all. But 'bound with common sense' is of more than figurative significance, for

Common Sense was the title of the pamphlet in which Paine defended American Independence.

And so to John Redman's codicil. Rarely can executors have been treated with such hale and hearty generosity:

> I desire and direct my executors to keep my dwelling house for at least a year after my decease, and also the same with my other house in Essex, and I do recommend them to visit Greensted Hall at least six times in that year, and to stop from Saturday to Monday morning, to hire a light coach and an able pair of horses, set out betimes and breakfast on the road, alternately to take one of their families, that each corner may be filled, to drink out the wine in the vault.
>
> The same to be observed in Hatton Garden; executors to order a dinner for themselves, half a score times; to consult and consider the business they have in hand, and not to spare the wine in the cellar, and the remainder at last to be divided between them and carried to their respective houses.

18

Bensusan: The Man and His Countryside

Essex has seen a number of distinguished writers make their homes, if only for a while, within its borders. Most have not been natives of the soil.

Conrad settled briefly by the Thames, at Stanford-le-Hope in a house called Ivy Walls, since demolished. At 'Comarques', a fine Georgian residence in Thorpe le Soken, Arnold Bennett wrote the third of his Clayhanger novels, *These Twain*. He went there in 1913 but sold the house seven years later, when he parted from his wife. He enjoyed yachting off the coast.

Tennyson spent some time at High Beach. Dorothy L. Sayers lived at 24 Newland Street, Witham, making it her home for twenty-eight years until her death in 1957. Another great novelist, H.G. Wells, occupied the old rectory at Little Easton for many years. A.J.A. Symons, best known for his biography of the enigmatic Frederick Rolf, *The Quest for Corvo*, resided until his death at Finchingfield, in Brick House by the pond.

There have been literary visitors as well. Among the regulars were Trollope, who came to hunt, and Charles Dickens, drawn by the then rural charm of Chigwell, which led him to use the King's Head as the model for 'The Maypole' in *Barnaby Rudge*. Mary E. Braddon did the same for Ingatestone Hall in her Victorian melodrama *Lady Audley's Secret*, a house she thinly camouflaged as Audley Court.

But our chief interest must be in those who more fully

'Godfreys', Langham, as Bensusan knew it

depicted the Essex scene, writers such as Henry Warren, who also lived at Finchingfield, and the Rev. Baring-Gould at Mersea, where he wrote *Mehalah*.

In *A Discovery of Old Essex* I devoted a page or so to S.L. Bensusan, whose association with Essex became so close that he is entitled to be dubbed an adopted son. Since then, my interest in the man and his countryside has grown apace. I have continued to collect his books as they make their sporadic appearances in second-hand bookshops, for all have long been out of print; and more and more I find myself in tune with his sentiments and values.

I write this as I pass my sixtieth year, and the conviction has long been growing that there are books which lie in wait for us on the far side of middle age, books which cannot speak to us while we are young. Among them I have come to place those written by Bensusan in his closing years. Although I greatly admire his Marshland stories, making him in a minor key 'the Thomas Hardy of Essex' (a comparison which embarrassed him), it is the more personal volumes which now so vitally appeal to me, produced at 'Godfreys' outside the village of Langham close by the Suffolk border. In these, written in seclusion on the edge of 'God's own county', he left a last will and testament, a vision of the good life which shines out bright and clear in our darkened age.

The books I have in mind are *Fireside Papers*, published by the Epworth Press in 1946 but written several years before; *Back of Beyond*, with a foreword dated 1945; *My Woodland Friends*, 1947; and *Quiet Evening*, 1950. These last three were published by Blandford Press. Each deals in the main with his life at Godfreys and the procession of the seasons there, with occasional glances over the shoulder at his former years. Any full account of those years, however, would require a study of his diaries and unpublished autobiography *Myself When Young*, held at the University of Essex.

Samuel Levy Bensusan was born in 1872. As his name readily tells us, he was of Jewish parentage. He was brought up in an orthodox household, his family being 'strictly observant Sephardic Jews'. Although he was to kick against the exclusiveness and restrictions of Judaism, there was one in the home who made a lasting impression on him in his boyhood. In his *Fireside Papers* he recalled with affection and understanding his blind and dying grandfather, who had been born in 1798 and who passed away at close on ninety. Bensusan remembered the old man in his bed, his lips reciting the Psalms, and wrote, 'The man who was the child turns to the Psalter too, as those now in the full flush of youth and vigour and indifference to all save mundane things, will turn in the years when all the daughters of music shall be brought low and the grasshopper shall be a burden and desire fail.' Lord Ernle's *The Psalms in Human Life* was one of those books Bensusan was always to treasure when so many others were left behind.

At first he planned to train for the Law, but ill health forced him to abandon that for free lance journalism, a career which was to last for more than forty years. He was the young editor of the *Jewish World* for 1897-8. However, his interest in religion soon widened into those of the East. He met Annie Besant, becoming a member of the Theosophical Society and an editor of its *Review*.

In the service of Fleet Street Bensusan was a music critic and contributed travel and countryside notes. His *Marshland Echoes* bears a dedication to H.A. 'Taffy' Gwynne, the editor of the *Morning Post*. He travelled widely in Britain and abroad and, in addition to articles, wrote books on diverse subjects, including *Home Life in Spain*, a book on Coleridge and another on the Renaissance of which he was the joint author. Although in his books he is very sparing in dropping names, he had more than a nodding acquaintance with many a famous figure in public life, and had for a brother-in-law a distinguished landscape painter. He had experience in government administration as well, as a civil servant in the Ministry of Agriculture.

During those active and crowded years his work kept him much in town, where he had rooms at the Temple, but always his eyes were upon the country scene, desiring some small stake in the land. He looked to Essex in particular and was to make four or five homes in the county.

In 1905 he met Lady Warwick at a garden party at her

home, Easton Lodge. It proved one of the key moments in his professional life, for it began a long association with 'Daisy', never dull and often exasperating. The following year he moved into the Brick House at Broxted near Great Easton. Here on the rolling land above the valley of the Chelmer he put down his roots for sixteen years, along with his wife Marion, the 'LA' (Local Authority) and 'CO' in his books. When they finally left, it was because he felt they had shaped their spot to completion and wanted another challenge. There was also 'a call to which it was necessary to respond'.

Bensusan's literary collaboration with the Countess of Warwick began in 1910 with her book on William Morris. He was her agent and adviser. For years he ghosted much of her work, beginning with the articles which appeared under her name in the *Daily Sketch*. Her second volume of memoirs, *Afterthoughts*, was very largely shaped by him, yet he was never credited in print for it.

Although he had written country stories before, the decisive breakthrough came in 1926 when he found his true *métier* with *Village Idylls*. This inaugurated his long series of books based on the age-old but fast-vanishing life of the Dengie hundred and the land around the Blackwater. I can but repeat what I have written before of his achievement in these volumes: 'He created tales based on the rural folk he knew at first hand ... all seen with a kindly eye and measured with an unerring instinct for the good and the true in their little worlds beyond the alien urban understanding.'

He wrote over 500 stories, the first being published in 1898. The locations he disguised as Maychester, Market Waldron, Tundon etc, but in the introduction to his *Marshland Omnibus* (Duckworth, 1954) he revealed the identity of a few.

Another of his retreats was in the very heart of 'the Denge'. In *Quiet Evening* he speaks of it as 'my first cottage'. It was Elizabethan, having the date of its erection on a beam in the living-room. The walls were panelled and there was an inglenook fireplace which in the 'victorious winters' often filled the room with smoke. There were no amenities: lighting was by oil lamps and candles;

drinking-water came by a carrier's cart; and there was no telephone. A postman called daily, complaining not only that the house was off his route, reached by a muddy track, but that the new owner had introduced letters into the remote corner. I have yet to learn just where this was but its being surrounded by a horseshoe moat should one day aid me in my search. It was two miles out from Southminster and rented for £10 a year.

His next Essex home was on the highway which follows the Blackwater between St Lawrence and Bradwell juxta Mare. This was Mote Cottage, substantial and white-weatherboarded, which stands right by the wayside with 'Cobbetts'. I can trace no details of his sojourn here in the 1920s, but the house seems to be the one he describes on page 138 of *Fireside Papers*: 'What a great relief to move to an upland cottage, though modern and not far removed from a villa. There was a garden, small and recently planted, on land that had in all probability been filched from the roadside waste. The air was fresh, the intermediate season brought no suggestion of ague, that old-time curse of the low-lying marshland. Tradesmen called, it was possible to get a paper by the afternoon, and you could walk without getting the stiff clay well over your boots. There was no moat complete with nightingale, but there were no rats either.'

The original of his character Father William was a next-door neighbour. According to Wentworth Day, the old man was removed to an institution where, within days, he lost the will to live. Bensusan was on holiday and was deeply grieved to find what had happened when he returned. As a Justice of the Peace with many years on the Bench, he might have been able to avert this sad end of a great character.

It was in 1932 that Bensusan and his CO discovered Godfreys. He was then nigh on sixty and was to remain there until the end in 1958. Not once in his books does he give it away by name, hiding it behind the fictitious name of 'Back of Beyond' and in his book with that title giving the most nebulous directions as to where it stood and how to get there. When I first went to the scattered parish of Langham in 1984, none of the few people I met on the lanes or at their doors had heard of Godfreys, nor even more regrettably of Bensusan himself. I was probably unlucky, but they led me to recall, perhaps unfairly, his lament on the new-style village life: 'The places of the old will be taken by the new folk who lack tradition, to whom the country is a playground and nothing more.' Always a jealous guardian of his privacy, and regarded by the old guard in the village with suspicion, a political heretic and a 'crank', all trace of him had seemingly been covered with a vengeance.

He was a connoisseur in his choice of friends and company, and there were types he could never freely mix with. Writing after eighteen years in the parish, under the heading of 'Retrospect' in *Quiet Evening*, he confesses: 'There is a village beyond my boundaries of which I know nothing, there are movements in which I take no part, interests that cannot be shared by those who do not kill for sport or drink for amusement or support policies of the day before yesterday. Perhaps my way of life is anti-social, but I cannot vary or mend it.' He had tried to get involved but had been rebuffed.

He added: 'When we came here I had certain ambitions, foremost among them to bring fertility to a forgotten or neglected hillside, to provide a sanctuary for persecuted wild life and in quietness, peace and beauty, to forget the stress and strain of the long years of hard work that had taken me over Southern Europe, North Africa, Western Asia and to America from Atlantic to Pacific.' And then, a page or so further on, he encapsulated in a sentence where his real contentment lay: 'Those of us whom life has disciplined obey instructions. Certain things remain; the pageant of the seasons, the study, the rare journeys to familiar haunts, the meeting with country men and women who belong to my time and face change with philosophy.'

Only after much wandering did I find the house, which I recognized, out in the fields at the end of a long track, from the photograph in *Fireside Papers* and a drawing by his illustrator, Joan Rickaby. The house then stood vacant and forlorn, which is not so now. A couple living within yards, Bensusan enthusiasts who dwelt upon what had been his land, confirmed that I had indeed found the elusive spot.

Bensusan has left on record how it looked when they first came upon it after a four-month search for a new home. It appealed at once, for it had what he called the necessary trinity of woodland, stream and meadow. The house, which had been thatched in remoter times, stands damp-free on a plateau of sand and gravel, with the land on one side falling away to a stream, Black Brook. The woods beyond and the larch grove close by the house have long since been greatly diminished by the axe.

Godfreys was built in the early years of the seventeenth century and had in turns been a farmhouse, a gamekeeper's cottage, a dwelling for farm labourers and at length the home of poultry-farmers. Simple and foursquare, when Bensusan arrived there were two rooms downstairs, one being a kitchen, and both with inglenooks. They were divided by a very narrow passage. Twisting stairs led to another two, and a second short flight gave access to the attics. Stone steps went down to a cellar. To the rear there was a shed with a bake oven.

The views were impeded by an army hut, sixty feet long, and many chicken sheds. Despite these eyesores and the twitch and the 'culch', the Bensusans could see the possibilities of the site. They had long experience in shaping recalcitrant soil to the inner eye. The 'Great Lady' driven here by her chauffeur and who looked askance upon the scene, I suspect was Lady Warwick.

Improvements were soon in hand, though proving long and costly. A porch was added to the house; a study replaced the bakery; and a conservatory went up. A summerhouse was erected among the larches (another in a woodland clearing pre-dated their arrival) and a little bridge made across the brook. As the years went by, an uneven croquet lawn materialized and conifers to break the wind about the house. Help was minimal. A gardener came in four days a week, and they employed an odd-job man from time to time.

In all, their domain extended to around fifty acres. Several of these consisted of the garden and the orchard created on the slope. Here, as part of 'the litany of green things growing', there were clematis, mimosa and a *prunus japonica*. Vegetables and fruit they produced in plenty, the surplus going to the local market. Much of the cultivation followed the esoteric guidelines of Rudolf Steiner, the planting of 'moon seeds' in particular. They also kept bees and reared pheasants, bringing the hens in among the chickens.

The woods lying beyond the meadows, which were leased to a farmer, accounted for another twenty acres. These and the creatures they harboured were Bensusan's first love, as the books he wrote in their presence repeatedly testify. He estimated that his trees ran to over thirty varieties, including the common oak, elm, ash, sycamore and larch, a few beeches and hornbeams, Spanish chestnut, the wild cherry and, a special delight, the mountain ash. Alders, but never enough for his satisfaction, lined the stream, and rhododendrons carpeted the earth in great abundance. Most of this woodland treasure was here when he arrived.

A bone of contention with some local people was Bensusan's total aversion to traps and guns, although in his younger days he had hunted game in Scotland and Africa, welcomed as he was then on the sidelines of Society. The Countess of Warwick had undergone a similar conversion.

In *Quiet Evening* he protests at wild life being 'butchered joyfully' and leaves his readers in no doubt about his revulsion for the hunt. 'Little owls and badgers, rare though they be, are not suffered to live.' He was careful not to spread the news abroad about the otters who were rare visitors to the brook. He looked with sorrow, too, on the violation of the landscape, the wholesale removal of hedgerows and the annihilation of insect life. 'The man who opposes modern methods and old cruelties,' he wrote, 'has a worthwhile job though he must not expect to escape rebuke, abuse or ostracism.' But there were times when he gave way to pressure, reluctantly allowing a pigeon shoot when the birds reached the proportions of a serious threat to neighbouring crops. Nature, he well knew, is red in tooth and claw, but he was loath to add to the suffering. He held in trust the hierarchy of life around him. It was wanton destruction he stood against – killing for 'fun' – and he deplored the lack of ecological vision. A tolerant and compassionate man, he gave vent to few recriminations, however. And this befitted one who walked the Middle Path.

They were halcyon days at Godfreys in the '30s. But then the shadows crept in, the losing battle with the body and the coming of war. His heart showed signs of weakness. His once keen senses now required glasses and a hearing aid, and neuritis settled in his writing hand. Yet his strength ebbed very slowly and he even welcomed 'Brother Fatigue'.

The darkness around his sanctuary is no more evident than in *Fireside Papers, A Countryman's Reflections*. On the title page he tells us it was 'Written by a log fire in a country cottage on the Essex-Suffolk border through night hours in 1942, 3, 4, while sirens wailed, searchlights probed, Luftwaffe raged and Huns imagined a vain thing.' It bears a strong sensation of finality, 'this little harvest of my years', though that was not quite yet to be. Although there is a measure of nostalgia, the book is governed by faith and hope.

With petrol rationed, distant excursions and guests were few and far between. Life centred more and more upon his study. 'I can't keep my pen from paper, it is the last surviving passion in a world grown grey.' He shared with the rest of the nation in those years an addiction to the news. Broadcasts, music and records of birdsong were among his consolations; in pre-war days he had played the discs in his woodland clearing. Through books he communed with 'the mighty dead'; the poets and Marcus Aurelius were never far away. 'Ultra-modernity' and writers and critics unrooted in the past were strictly taboo.

Outside, his peace and seclusion were invaded. A searchlight battery arrived. Then Land Girls followed. Three thousand larches had to come down for pit-props, leaving barely fifty. Some splendid oaks were felled in error. A flying bomb, the doodlebug, plunged into other trees and inflicted wounds upon the house. Overhead, he heard each night the shattering roar of planes as they made their way to Europe from the airfield two miles away at Boxted. One jettisoned its petrol tanks into the wood; another came down, its pilot safe, to plough among the precious hornbeams. The American base became operational in May 1943 and was noted for its Mustangs and P47 Thunderbolts.

Amid these scars of war, his spirit, though often troubled,

stayed remarkably serene. And when the war was over and all the privations in its aftermath, Godfreys again became a place 'where peace comes dropping slow'. Once more Bensusan could contemplate in stillness the wheeling seasons and the lives of the creatures and plants about him. More than ever at this time he could have said with Vita Sackville-West, 'The country habit has me by the heart.'

His severance from the affairs of men was now all but complete. Like all of us in due time, he was becoming one of yesterday's men. Like few of us, he savoured to the full the present moment despite the shadow of what he called 'the Bad Companion'.

Quiet Evening was virtually his 'last of the summer wine'. He had eight years to go before he died at the age of eighty-six. He had a firm conviction in an after-life, in a plurality of lives, in fact, for he believed in the long journey of the spirit, and in Karma. I hope his faith has been confirmed; and if there is a beyond, as I suspect, I hope, too, he is now creating astral gardens ever closer to his heart's desire.

19

Through Essex in 1900

The radical difference between the life and look of Essex today and as it was at the turn of the century, cannot be better appreciated than by reading some of the travel and tourist accounts written at that time. There are three books on my shelves which reveal this in particular: Rider Haggard's *Rural England*, Reginald A. Beckett's *Romantic Essex* and a slender guidebook, *New Holidays in Essex, with Rail and Walking Routes, Boating, Fishing and Shooting Notes*, edited by Percy Lindley.

Rider Haggard's book is a solo *tour de force* and its character would surprise many readers, for he is best known to the public at large as the author of *King Solomon's Mines*, *She*, and other tales of high adventure in Africa. In fact, his range of interests was wide. He wrote several books on rural economy, including *The Poor and the Land*, for which he was made a Knight Commander of the British Empire, and he excelled as a Norfolk farmer.

Rural England is a massive two-volume work, reaching to 1,200 pages. Printed by Longmans in 1902, it originated as a series of articles for the *Daily Express*. The great depression in agriculture was then at its height. With such eminent examples before him as Arthur Young and Cobbett, he set out with a companion to journey through twenty-seven English counties, an intensive, arduous excursion which took eight months to complete. It was not his aim to describe the historic or the picturesque – although they figure in parenthesis – but to sample and record at first hand the state of farming and the attendant social conditions in the villages. It is a gloomy picture in the main which he unfolds, and his

Farm labourers' treehouse in 1900

conclusions with his remedies for the distress, a national shame and folly, make absorbing reading even now, in our age of high yields, surpluses and Technology the lord of the land. The chapter on Essex, based on 150 notes he compiled along the way, can be found in Volume I.

Labour here was not so much scarce as generally low in quality. Nevertheless, London and its growing eastern suburbs were exerting an insidious pull. In the hierarchy of rural management he found the landowners to be in the least envied position, with very low returns from their estates. Much of the farmland was let for very small rents. But there was additional income to be had from leasing shooting rights. Haggard noted that tenant farmers were better off, for although labour was proving dear, fewer men need be employed. It was the labourers who were collectively doing best of all. Earnings averaged 18 shillings to £1 a week, which sounds abnormally little to us, but food was cheap and abundant. Rents were also low for cottages. Against this, Haggard found very many of these dwellings to be well below standard. Yet despite the poor housing, by and large the population in the countryside was healthy, a major exception being those who toiled on the marshlands, where the ague was rife.

Periods of grim weather were one of the major factors for the sorry state of things. I gave some instances in my previous book. Rider Haggard mentions the great gale of 1897:

> Not far from Burnham on Crouch we saw a tract of country that through the breach of the sea wall ... was flooded with salt water to the extent of several thousand acres. Indeed, some of it is still so flooded by every tide, since in the present depressed state of agriculture nobody seems able or willing to find the money to make sound the defences. The aspect of the land is most curious – as though it had been swept by fire. There stand the fences black and dead, and from them rise the stark, gaunt trees. The soil also is 'black like pitch when wet and like cinders when dry', as one farmer described it to me; indeed, the place appears a home of death and desolation. Even if the money were forthcoming to restore it to fertility, to do so would be the work of many years.

Rider Haggard also remarked on the abnormally long drought of 1901. He was told of a pond usually seventeen feet deep where there was not a pailful of water left. In the region of Ardleigh, always one of the driest parts of the county, 'practically no rain had fallen for five years.' The cloud was plentiful – 'Essex shows' – but failed to deliver.

Haggard went to each area of the county, each marked

with the individuality of its soil. At Great Braxted he was struck by the remarkable length of the wall which encloses the estate. 'What must it have cost, I wonder? The dates upon the wall show it was built in or about 1827, when corn was so high, and labour so cheap, and Essex landowners could afford to spend thousands to ensure a completer privacy. They could scarcely do it now, poor folk, that is, if they look to the land for a living. Since I saw it I have received a letter from Mr Henry Siggins, who tells me that this wall was built by his father and grandfather for the late Peter Du Cane, Esq.' They must have been the foremen, for it took many hands to erect the wall, which stretches for close on four miles.

At Maldon, once surrounded by wheat-growing country of the finest kind, he noted 'thousands of acres which can only be described as derelict. In 1901, at any rate, few of the fields seemed to produce a crop of grass high enough to hide a lark.'

He spent a very full day out in the Rodings, travelling around by motor car and driven, somewhat recklessly it seems, by a well-known gentleman of the Essex Hounds who addressed the vehicle as though it were a horse. The Rodings much appealed to Haggard as it has to so many others, then and now. After remarking on the heavy nature of the soil, 'admirably suited to the growth of wheat', he wrote of 'its lack of timber, its dearth of houses, and its complete sequestration from the world. Although it lies within thirty miles of London I do not think I have visited any place in England that impressed me as so utterly rural, so untouched by the push and bustle of our age.' It is a worthy exaggeration and still holds good in the urbanized Essex of today.

While in the neighbourhood he visited Waples Mill, farmed by Isaac Mead, the Essex Lad I wrote about some pages back. Mead was not at home, but his wife showed Haggard round the hundred acres held from University College.

Several success stories of a major kind emerged from Rider Haggard's tour. He met the Hon. Edward Strutt of Terling, brother of Lord Rayleigh, 'one of the most skilful farmers in England' who farmed 10,000 acres and had created a celebrated dairy herd. His accounts and records were thorough and systematic to the last detail. 'Never before,' Haggard wrote, 'had I seen such books as those that he keeps.'

Tiptree Fruit Farm, under the energetic management of Mr Wilkin, was also outstanding, despite the effect of drought. In 1901 it had supplied jam to close on 10,000 customers. But perhaps the venture which most caught Haggard's imagination was the Salvation Army Colony at Hadleigh by the Thames. Although he was unable to include it in his itinerary, he did get an interview with General Booth, and his account of their conversation runs to ten pages. Booth's diagnosis of the national ills and his ideas for their amelioration were broadly in accord with the views of the author.

'The object of this colony,' Haggard informed his readers, 'is to give employment, with food and lodging in return for his labour, to any able-bodied man who is willing to work, irrespective of the nationality or creed of the applicant. All sorts of agriculture, stock and poultry rearing, brick making, etc, are there carried on with considerable success. There are 1,280 acres of farm land, 300 acres under fruit and market-gardening, and seventy acres given up to industrial undertakings. The first cost of the freehold land, together with that of planting orchards, was £40,390, but in addition I gather that £60,000 or £70,000 have been invested in buildings, brickworks, machinery, wharves, barges, stock, etc.'

More can be learned about this commune from other and later sources. *Kelly's Directories* in the 1930s tell us that Hadleigh House and the ruined castle then belonged to the Salvation Army, 'the principal landowners .... The Farm Colony situated here was founded by the first General Booth, both as a philanthropic and a commercial enterprise, and since its commencement some eight thousand men have been benefited by a residence here. The colony now comprises about 2,000 acres of arable and pasture land and foreshore in Hadleigh and Leigh parishes, including the fishing rights at Hadleigh Ray; large brickfields exist on the estate, and there are over 100 acres of orchard ground.' But its role had greatly changed since 1900. 'The Colony is now being used for the training in agriculture of lads who intend emigrating to Canada, Australia and New Zealand.' A conspicuous feature of the landscape was an elaborate tramway linking the farm with the shore. The colony no longer exists.

These undertakings are among the few bright spots on Haggard's pages. Mostly his narration tells of struggle and apprehension. Among the most memorable reports is one on his visit to a farmer in the vicinity of Waltham. I give it unedited for its telling detail and for his reaction to what he saw.

I asked him of his labour, and was rewarded by a strange discovery. He was employing twenty hands at an average weekly wage of 18s to £1, some of whom we saw at work. As he was without cottage accommodation on the farm, I enquired where these men lodged. He answered 'In one of the buildings'. I asked to see the place, and was shown a brick shed, measuring twelve or fourteen square feet, which might have served as a wagon house, and was, I think I am right in saying, windowless. In this place, upon sacks that were laid round the walls, slept the twenty men upon the floor. No washing apparatus was visible and no fireplace. [But an even more disturbing sight was to follow.]

About a hundred yards away, on the slope of a hill, stands a hollow elm, at the foot of which were the ashes of a fire and an iron rod used to support the cooking pot. Round about lay some boughs, which served as benches. This was at once the kitchen and the parlour of the twenty men, who winter and summer did their cooking and spent their Sundays and leisure hours with no other shelter than that old tree afforded – or so I was informed. Any who are interested in the matter of rural accommodation may study the details of this delectable resort in the accompanying photograph, which was taken by ourselves. These labourers, by the way, were all casuals, and presumably unmarried; but their employer said that some of them had been with him as long as three years.

Let the reader realise the position. It meant that the men, twenty, or perhaps less of them in the winter, within thirty miles of London, existed, and I presume still exist, at all seasons of the year in a fashion that the lowest Kaffirs would refuse. Their sleeping place, a crowded shed, their bedding, sacks, their shelter by day, a tree, their food such as unskilled hands can cook in an iron pot, their female society none, their recreation the beer-house, where, as their master told me, they spent most of their good wages; their refuge in sickness the public infirmary, to which when I was at the place one of them had just been taken. Had I not seen it with my own eyes I would not have believed that such a state of affairs was possible. And yet who is to be blamed? Not the farmer, as he had at most but one cottage on his holding. The landlord? Very probably he could not afford to build, and knew nothing of the matter. The men? Work was plentiful; they might go elsewhere if they liked, but so far as I was able to discover were satisfied with their lot. The problem is too hard for me. Of one thing only I am certain: it is not right that in a highly civilised country human beings should pass their lives under conditions that must be as comfortless and insanitary as they are degrading.

Such news from the countryside is heard no more. But the counterpart can yet be found in the poverty traps of our inner cities. The poet's warning still rings clear:

> Ill fares the land, to hastening ills a prey
> Where Wealth accumulates and Men decay.

Rural England is not solely a magnificent piece of first-hand observation and reporting. It stands as the testament of one man's social concern and humanism. Never once in his forest of facts did he lose sight of individual people. So before we leave him for my other witnesses to Essex around 1900, let me give you a final instance of this, an example of his compassionate understanding of old-time folk. Again, I shall give his own words almost in full measure, for this is one book by Rider Haggard, a rarity, which is not likely to come your way.

Not far from Blunt's Hall [a farm belonging to Edward Strutt] I saw an old labourer named John Lapwood, whose life experience, which I verified by inquiry, is worth preserving. For half a century or more he worked on the Post Hall and Oliver Farms in Witham, and now, by the help of some friends, was spending his last days in a little cottage, where he lived with his old wife. We found him – an aged and withered but still apple-cheeked individual – seated upon a bank 'enjoying of the sweet air, although it be a bit draughty'. He told me that in his young days wages for horsemen used to be down to 9s a week, and for daymen to 8s, when the weather allowed them to be earned. During the Crimean War bread cost him a shilling a loaf, and other food a proportionate price. He stated that for months at a time he had existed upon nothing but a diet of bread and onions, washed down, when he was lucky, with a little small-beer. The onions he ate until they took the skin off the roof of his mouth, blistering it to whiteness, after which he was obliged to soak them in salt to draw the 'virtue' out of them. They had no tea, but his wife imitated the appearance of that beverage by soaking a burnt crust of bread in boiling water. On this diet he became so feeble that the reek of the muck which it was his duty to turn, made him sick and faint; and often, he said, he would walk home at night from the patch of ground where he grew the onions and some other vegetables, with swimming head and uncertain feet. I asked if his children, of whom there were eight, lived on onions also. He answered no, they had generally a little cheese and butter in the house, but he could not put it into his own stomach when they were hungry and cried for food. 'Things is better now' he added.

There is barely a shadow of these things in the next of my books from the past. It is pre-eminently a celebration of the marriage between scene and history.

This is Beckett's *Romantic Essex* (and how ironic that would have sounded to old John Lapwood). It is sub-titled 'Pedestrian Impressions'. Every few months I go to it again, for it is not just a fine old travelogue on the county, but literature in the worthiest sense of the word, even though at times the prose may be somewhat too flowery for modern taste. 'Topography is for me a branch of autobiography,' Beckett wrote in the opening chapter. There have been better guidebooks to Essex since, better in being tighter in plain facts and much more of them. Nor does it reach the literary standard of, say, Henry Warren's *Essex*. Yet it is pervaded by the spirit of place and, just as importantly, that of the author. It has style and is a book which endears by its contemplative approach. Much that I have collected down the years I would part with, if I had to, but not this small and now scarce volume.

Mine is the second edition of July 1907. It lacks the three painter-etchings reproduced in the first, of 1901, but this is offset by a frontispiece photograph of the old Green Man at Finchingfield, an inn which went by fire early in 1905. In his Prefatory Note, the author writes: 'I am consoled by thinking that the old house is saved from possible future profanation.' He had once stayed there, and writing that line in far-off Budapest, 'my present place of exile', we can sense his regret at its going. Another Green Man stands there now.

The title page is inviting. 'Romantic Essex' is printed in red, and below the author's name is a tiny drawing of an ornate sundial. Should you wonder why he gave his book this title, a quote from Walter Pater on the page makes the choice clear: 'The addition of strangeness to beauty constitutes the romantic.' This is applicable to Essex, if by strange we mean the unfamiliar, for when Beckett wrote, so much of the county lay unknown to outsiders. His was one of the books which opened up Essex, especially for Londoners, when wages and holiday aspirations were far more modest. The focal point for travel now has switched to wider horizons. Beaches with sure sunshine have become the vogue. Essex is merely on the doorstep and too domestic.

Reginald Beckett was not a resident here, and I can tell you nothing of his life and background. But of the man, his tastes, his temperament and values, the book speaks readily. In advance, he thanks his readers for not being 'deterred by an unpromising subject or the amateur craftsmanship of an unknown writer'. His book helped to remove the stigma of dullness from 'flat' Essex, revealing 'the mystery which underlies the obvious'. He was well able to substantiate his claim that, 'For variety of interest, and for a certain homelike sweetness which excites not only admiration but affection, Essex bears the palm.' In the first two chapters he prepares the way with his philosophy on travel, extolling the merits of walking, of footpaths and green lanes. Then, having put his armchair reader in receptive mood, he is off

on his excursions, devoting each chapter to a choice location
or ranging through a wider district.

Keeping in mind my purpose to highlight the contrast
between then and now, there is much in the book which
need not beg attention here, for thankfully not everything
has changed beyond all recognition in the landscape. But
before I select a few things from his pages, something must
be shown of his recurring theme of hospitality.

Everywhere he went he found a friendly people and more
than once rested his feet in a carrier's cart. There was always,
it seems, a welcome at a farmhouse or a cottage door. He
must have had the knack of brushing aside suspicion.

Who takes a holiday in the Rodings now? One summer
he and his family stayed at an ancient farmhouse there,
'where nearness to London is not to be measured by miles'.
He concealed its name and position but with a few strokes of
the pen unfolded, scene by scene, the final setting.

> Following a faint track slant-wise across the grass, you go
> through a little wicket and across a footbridge, which leads
> you over a deep, grassy ditch. The latter, from its rectangular
> form, you perceive to be the remains of a moat which
> formerly protected the house. The ample proportions of the
> building are in keeping with its ancient dignity. The
> house-door stands open and reveals to you, beyond the hall,
> which is paved with tiles and panelled with dark polished oak
> from floor to ceiling, a glimpse of sunlit garden beyond the
> further bank of the moat. If you pass through, and then
> glance up at the house, the old-world aspect of the place is
> even more striking; for the slightly cold and formal lines of
> the front have given place to bold projecting gables and
> massive chimney-stacks ....

Then follows a description of idyllic, hot August afternoons
spent in the surrounding countryside, in the harvest fields or
by a shaded river, watching the roach 'slide out from the
weeds and lie luxuriously in the sunlit water where it flowed
pellucid over the gravel'.

In the evenings they returned to the house they came to
regard as home. 'As we fell asleep at night in an exquisitely
fresh white room, we would hear the cry of the owl in the
great barn, and be wakened in the morning by the plaintive

cooing of wood pigeons .... Such are the peaceful signs that mark the passage of the hours in an Essex farmhouse of the olden time.'

He writes as though he guards a magic place against the world, a secret house and garden. Where could that house have been, and is it still there, one of those dotted about the land in those tranquil parts? If it yet stands, no doubt a hundred years have changed it, although perhaps it is not too much in disguise. Despite the author's vagueness, I nourish a lurking hope that someday I may find it, discovered by a stray clue or a quirk of fate.

Another time he was 'in a beautiful district near Stow Maries' when a storm arose. 'As the storm bursts we are glad to take shelter in a neighbouring cottage. Tea is in progress; we are invited to share it, and hospitably made at home. So we sit by the open door, inhaling the fresh air of the revived vegetation, while the lightning flashes across the wooded landscape, and the thunder rolls gradually away.'

There is nothing grand in these remembered moments, yet they have an intimacy which lasts. Some of us will recall the like in Essex, and not so many years ago. But gone are the days, to my regret, when bed and breakfast could be found at random on many a lane. This age of universal motoring, with the near-eclipse of walking and the touring bike, has meant goodbye to all that. Instead, most whisk by and through, missing the green minutiae. What lies beyond the windscreen is a blur and a ribbon of road to be traversed. At best it is out and home in a day. The square mile is rarely explored in depth and with close enjoyment.

Inns, too, have changed; many are no longer the hostelries that Beckett knew. At Dedham he put up at the Marlborough Head, where accommodation can still be had. The room in which he slept 'had a curiously carved beam running diagonally across the ceiling, and it is supposed that this part of the house was open on two sides to the street, and supported at the angle by a wooden pillar'. He also stayed at the Bell in Castle Hedingham, in an upstairs room which ran the whole length of the front. Among others, he dined in St Anne's Castle at Great Leighs and in the Griffin on Danbury Hill.

At the Ferry Boat, North Fambridge, he saw a famished multitude. 'The civil landlord told me that these people, who drift all through the summer from one farm to another, wherever there is work to be got, had come into this out-of-the-way place without any provision having been made for them. His wife had gone with a cart to a neighbouring village, and presently returned with some loaves of bread; after which the tumult subsided a little, and I was furnished with a meal in comfortable quarters usually sacred to the Fambridge Yacht Club.'

This is one of the very few notices Beckett gives of the privations which could be found. It was here, too, at Fambridge, that he saw the effects of the flood in 1897. He tells how, when a government inspector, an army man, was sent to view the damage in these lonely parts, he had to ask the name of the river (the Crouch, of course) for he had never heard of it. That must have been passed around with gusto among the villagers.

While on the marshlands, Beckett went to Wakering Stairs and looked out to the Maplin Sands. He did not hazard the Broomway, the track to Foulness, having been there once before, but at the Stairs he witnessed 'one of the most curious sights I have ever beheld' just before dusk. It was then 'there appeared a procession of market carts rapidly driven across the sands, amid much splashing, through water about a foot deep, with two or three fishing-smacks beyond and a distant steamer on the horizon.' The military are in occupation now, and this muddy, low-tide route, lying with 'broomstick' markers off the shore, has long been forbidden for civilian use. The major and dramatic exception was during the great flood disaster of 1953. (Should you want a fuller account of Foulness as it was, you could not do better than seek out Herbert W. Tompkins' *Marsh-Country Rambles* published in 1904 by Chatto & Windus.)

When Beckett passed through Ingatestone in that year of 1897, he saw evidence of the summer hailstorm, no harvest being reaped. At that time the Petre family was still at Thorndon, and Ingatestone Hall was occupied by several Roman Catholic families. At South Weald his attention was aroused by 'an inn with the pictorial sign of the *Golden Fleece*, spacious and quaint, but fallen upon evil days'. The Fleece is still with us, on the highway to Brentwood, but is now a pub which has been totally refurbished. At nearby Pilgrims Hatch his eye was taken with 'a curious post-office in the side of a farmhouse'. It was while walking from here, and reaching a point between Margaretting and Stock, that he asked a young fellow the way. The lad was pushing himself along in a wheelbarrow. 'Follow the telegrams,' came the reply, by which he meant the telegraph poles.

He visited Laindon and saw the Fortune of War, the original inn, which in this day houses a printing business. It stands at the bottom of Noak Hill out of Billericay, at the intersection with the old Laindon High Road. This should not be confused with the later pub which took the name, by the roundabout on the A127. More recently this has become the Hustlers, large and garish.

Beckett thought the Fortune of War derived its name from Sir John Hawkwood, 'who held land near here', but this assertion I cannot verify. When our traveller was there, small-scale festivities were under way in a field near the inn. 'I was told that this was Fortune Fair, a yearly event since time immemorial.' It was clearly a custom that was fast dying out. A few lines further on he tells of knocking at a cottage after dark, requesting a drink of water. The occupants stared at him with incredulity. 'In the lonely hills near Laindon,' he observed, 'the people are still very primitive.'

It is time for me to close on Reginald Beckett, but at no better spot than Finchingfield, that showpiece of north Essex. He arrived in a carrier's wagon, on a clear, cold, moonlit evening in September. The lamps were being lit in the cottage windows. He descended in the stable yard of the Green Man. Once inside, 'With the ready freemasonry of country inns, we were forthwith installed into the best that the house could bestow.' When morning came, from the gabled window of his room he had a bird's-eye view of the village, a memorable picture then as now. The sign of the inn hung in a fine and ancient frame, iron scrollwork, the product of some former blacksmith.

The brick bridge with its single arch remains, of course.

The church on the hill is also in all essentials just the same. But it is precisely here that the past is another country. So many churches today have been forced through vandalism to lock their doors. This is even so for those in rural isolation. How ironic, then, it is for us, when Beckett pauses in his praise to say: 'The church – thanks to a laudable and happily growing practice – stands always open.'

What it lacks in the pensive style and meandering approach of Reginald Beckett, *New Holidays in Essex* – price 6d – makes up for with its compact, detailed information. Yet it is not without a lyrical aside. It is very short, just seventy pages of small print, and thin enough to be slipped into a pocket. Severely restricted in scope, it plots four routes through southern Essex, using the railways as the link from Brentwood to the coast.

The guide, with stations, mileages and recommended walks and prospects, was designed to lure out Londoners to the 'fresh fields' and breezy seashores within an hour by train from the metropolis. Quite apart from being a tourist profile of these parts as they were in the last years of Victoria's reign, it would merit inclusion in any museum of travel.

The outward bound begins in Brentwood High Street with a Dickensian touch. At the famous old coaching inn, the galleried White Hart, we are treated to reminiscences of an aged ostler 'grown white in the service':

I remember it well when I were a boy, and most of the coaches on the road used to change horses here. It were 'four up' and 'four down' all day long; there weren't much quiet then; plenty to do and plenty to get for that matter, for the tips came pretty often. Seventy-two coaches passed the old house in the twenty-four hours; them was lively times. I can well remember when fifty coach-horses and upwards were kept in these stables, beside fifteen 'posters', and postboys booted and spurred, always ready to start on the call of 'next turn'. Yes, and I remember them galleries when they were crowded with travellers, servants and luggage, very different to their deserted look nowadays. Who'd have thought people would ever travel behind an iron horse.

The White Hart has very different customers now. But even in 1900 the rural atmosphere was going, so that the guidebook had to say, 'Enough remains of old Brentwood to give it a cheerful air of age; not of ancient Brentwood, for that is almost "improved" away.'

To the south there were the pleasures of Thorndon Hall with its wooded park two miles in length. There were footpaths from Herongate and Ingrave, although the choicest northern part could be entered only with the written permission of Lord Petre. This was needed, as well, to visit the chapel and the gallery of paintings. The mortuary chapel on the edge of an oak wood also gets a mention. (Not long before writing this, I heard a news report that two skulls left outside an Essex police station had been found to have come from there!)

The Hall has now been converted to luxury flats. The building is not the original. That stood a mile and a half away. Acquired by the Petres in 1573, it was remodelled by the first Lord, John. The eighth Lord Petre, Robert James, a noted landscape gardener and botanist, commenced to change the Tudor house to the Palladian style. But after his death through smallpox in 1743, his son, Robert Edward, pulled it down and built the present mansion. It suffered much in the fire of 1878, and after the First World War the family went back to where their fortunes started, to Ingatestone.

Weald Hall with its belvedere was standing when the guide was written. The Kembles, too, were at Runwell. The rector then of that parish was the Rev. T.C. Webster, 'the popular lecturer on Songs and Singing, or how Character is formed by Song'.

One of the most impressive of views in Essex is that to the south from Laindon or Langdon Hills, from One Tree Hill in particular, even though it is marred by installations and other developments along the river. The book quotes a description by a Mr Hissey who paid a summer visit. It is one of exuberant extravagance.

> It is astonishing that a spot of so much beauty (possessing a peculiar character all its own, and not to be repeated in

England) should be so near to town and so little known ....
From where we stood we looked down through the sun-filled
air upon a glorious expanse of waving woods, green
meadows and red tilled fields, down upon miles of smiling
verdure, dotted here and there with scattered farmsteads,
red-roofed villages, and ever and again a peep of a distant
church tower or spire. All this goodly prospect, bounded
only by the circling blue of the far-away horizon, where land
and sky were blended together in a dim, dreamy uncertainty.
Right through the heart of this map-like panorama wound
the silvery Thames, or so it looked to us ... our vision
rejoiced in its unaccustomed freedom, confined as it is for so
great a portion of the year to the sadly limited vista of a
London street ....

There is more, but to cap it all the writer ends with a touch of
near-ludicrous hyperbole, declaring that the uninterrupted
view 'gives a sense of vastness to the scene more suggestive
of Western America, that land of big rivers, mighty
distances and broad effects'.

Mr Hissey was not alone in uttering such fulsome praise.
Hope-Moncrieff writing in his *Essex* (published in 1926)
regretfully observed: 'Arthur Young and other writers of his
time grew enthusiastic over the view from Langdon Hills;
but how many West-end Londoners today know this height
even by name, and why does no poet here supply me with a
burst of quotation?' Presumably, East Enders knew it well.

Maldon and the valley of the Blackwater are featured well
in the guidebook. Osea Island has not altered much, with its
'Robinson Crusoe sense of ease'. Just two or three decoy
ponds out of the one-time score or so were being worked in
the area. Since then they have joined the others as curiosities.

The boating facilities were much commended. There was a
choice of sailing boats, like the *Lark* and the *Matilda*, open
craft and punts, also locally called 'canoes'. Once on board,
there was a standard item in the diet. 'The Maldon sausage
may be approached with a child-like trust ... on more than
one cruise, after figuring at three meals, the writer has heard
a clamorous cry for more sausages for tea.' Among the fish
to be had, the conger eels were sometimes very large. 'On
Dec 15th 1887, a conger 6 feet long, and weighing 55 lbs,

was caught by a dredgerman.' The North Sea then was unknown by that name, being the German Ocean until the 1914-18 war.

Burnham was especially singled out for its boating and fishing, its wild-fowl and, above all, its oysters, for you could eat the finest 'natives' as they came into the boat – that is, if you were 'fortunate enough to know an owner generous enough to invite you to such a feast'. Hardly a treat in store for day or weekend trippers. Among its merits, Burnham, we are told, would prove 'a place which none of your friends have been to, and you can talk safely about it as though you had known it all your life'.

There are many little pointers in Percy Lindley's book to places which had a truly rustic character. Some of the drawings are vividly evocative of this. But by way of conclusion – for this chapter has proved a lengthy circuit in itself – I open his pages on Danbury and Little Baddow, a most distinctive corner of the county, with leafy heights and 'Devonshire-like lanes'.

As in *Romantic Essex*, the Griffin gets a mention: 'The straggling one street of Danbury, with its houses raised on banks on each side of the road, is not unlike an Ardennes village. Five minutes to the left from the Green is the Griffin, an ancient inn happily unspoiled by modern improvements. It is the quiet summer quarters of a few well-known English artists and others who delight in the pastoral country round about.' Beckett judged it 'one of the oldest and best inns in Essex'. Now newly appointed and with a restaurant, it maintains an excellent standard in the medium price range.

Two other pubs are named downhill at Little Baddow: the General's Arms and the Rodney, which provided for picnic parties. Both are still thriving.

One final reference brings me very close to home. Great Baddow, two miles away from my cottage, is described as 'a remote looking little village ... prettily hidden among trees', its church with a 'handsome ivy-covered tower'. Once a fashionable place of residence with an air of gentility, this cannot be said of the 'village' in this year of grace. The ivy on the church has gone and so, too, has any feeling of remoteness here. On its northern side, Great Baddow has merged with Chelmsford's suburbs. With the coming of the new by-pass, the southern route around the county town, the few remaining contours of 1900 have been further erased.

The year 2000 stares us in the face.

20

The 'Haunting' of Bower House

I began this book with graves and I end with a tale of 'ghosts'. You will note the inverted commas, for although it is a true story I have to tell, based upon my personal inquiry and the records I kept at the time, I continue to question, as I questioned then, the meaning of the events.

I must at the outset declare my attitude to the so-called supernatural, which I prefer to call, more neutrally, the paranormal. It is one of qualified belief tempered by scepticism. There are phenomena, ESP and the like, whose reality has been settled to my satisfaction. To the naïve materialist, 'in the prison of one thought', I would say with Hamlet: 'There are more things in heaven and earth than are dreamed of in your philosophy.' But although I have no doubt that there are intimations of immortality in our lives, I have long chosen to walk the razor's edge between reasoned hope and evidence. This is particularly so in dealing with specific case histories of psychic experience which so often present a tangled web. It is not easy to stay out coldly in a no-man's land, with the will to believe on one side and the equally powerful wish not to believe on the other.

Essex has its quota of haunted houses, traditional and contemporary, the most celebrated – or, as some would have it, notorious – being Harry Price's much publicized Borley Rectory, which ended its days being gutted by fire. The house I write of here had a brief history far more modestly intriguing. For myself, I neither saw nor heard anything untoward. Instead, my role was one of a sympathetic 'detective'.

Twenty-six years ago, at a time when I was still a member

Bower House, Havering-atte-Bower

of the Society for Psychical Research, I was shown an article in a local newspaper boldly headed 'He's Waiting For A Ghost'. It was a colourful piece of reporting, written, as I was later to learn, to be in tune with the season, one of dark winter days with Christmas on the horizon. Its subject was an alleged haunting of Bower House at Havering near Romford; the appearance of an apparition to two former caretakers of the property. The figure was identified as the phantom of one Lucy Baynes, 'a girl who died a tragic death more than 200 years ago'. The feature also asserted that others employed in the house had had experiences of a similar nature.

Bower House, a red-brick mansion of over thirty rooms, occupies a prominent position in extensive, open grounds on the upper slopes of Orange Tree Hill. Not far to the north is the highest point in the surrounding countryside, over 300 feet. The original house of five bays was built in 1729 for

John Baynes. The single-storeyed wings, canted towards the south, were added about 1800. On the north side is the Bell House with a central lantern, the former livery stables.

Within Bower House itself, there is an imposing entrance hall. Here there is an inscription with the words: 'From the remains of the Royal Palace of Havering Bower, situated on the summit of the hill, this dwelling was founded by John Baynes, Sergeant-at-Law, so that he might retire into sure ease and have pleasure for himself and his friends. A.D. 1729. H. Flitcroft was architect. C. Bridgeman designer. The Arms of King Edward III sculptured on this stone are sufficient proof of its antiquity.' The arms are original, taken from the old palace. In the wing leading off the hall, there is a wide staircase flanked with gloomy paintings by Thornhill. At the head of the main flight, and well above the small landing, the wall is pierced by a large window which floods the staircase with light. It is here, her hand on the bannisters, that 'Lucy' is said to have appeared.

On the ground floor, the main room, No. 13, is hung with a number of old portraits. One is of Lucy Baynes, 'the sole surviving daughter of John'. Over her dress is a purple sash and she holds an orange. Another is of a bearded man, in early middle age I should judge. He is dressed in black and has a large, white collar. This is the brother, referred to in the newspaper as 'a Quaker', presumably because of his garb.

In daylight the house looks sober and pleasant enough. This did not do for the reporter, however, looking for good copy. 'Bower House stands gaunt, empty and forbidding', once the home of a family 'whose ancestry shows one of stark tragedy, insanity and bitter sadness – the remorse that calls Lucy, the teenage daughter, and her brother, back from the grave .... AT THE RIGHT OF A SHORT GREEN LAY THE HOUSE – EERIE, SILENT, STILL.' Good atmospheric stuff, although not having seen any records on the family, I cannot vouch for the 'stark tragedy', and Lucy's brother certainly played no part in the reputed haunt. (Reading this, I was reminded of Thomas de Quincey's candid observation in his essay on Joan of Arc: 'On a fine breezy forenoon I am audaciously sceptical, but as twilight sets in my credulity grows steadily till it becomes equal to anything that could be desired.') The house was indeed then empty, vacated by Ilford Ltd and awaiting possession by Ford's as a training centre.

Having seen the article and my interest being aroused, I arranged to visit the house, accompanied by a friend who was another journalist on the self-same paper. But from the very beginning problems began to accumulate.

Two months had passed since the story had been printed, and the first witness quoted was dead. This was the caretaker, Mr R,* 'a strong-willed, honest, hard-working man'. This is how his involvement was reported.

He told his mate, Mr D, who was to prove his successor, that he had heard footsteps on the stairs and then seen the ghost of Lucy, recognized from the portrait. His dog had sprung up and gone wild. R then went to the local pub, where he was known. He entered 'pale and shivering ... his face white, his eyes showing fear, and his voice cracked'. A few weeks later, he died from a heart attack. His family did not take kindly to the implications in what they saw as a garbled story, and since it was becoming a sensitive issue, I decided not to contact his wife or visit the publican.

Mr D also claimed to have seen the ghost in period dress. The article described him as 'a quiet, matter-of-fact man' who spoke of himself as having 'nerves of steel'. He had been about to speak to her when he sensed she was no ordinary person. The air was cold. 'I called to her; she disappeared.' His employment as caretaker was brief.

I wrote to Mr D at home and sent him a lengthy questionnaire. I never had a reply. Perhaps my list of close on thirty questions looked too precise and formidable, for few caretakers can be literary people. Perhaps, too, he felt intimidated and put on the spot. Going in full sail was a mistake I now regret.

I was able to see much of the interior when I made my visit. We were taken on a conducted tour by a caretaker, Mr N, who had taken over in the New Year. Very talkative and somewhat histrionic (he was once a small-part actor), he

---

* I shall give initials rather than the names of all those involved, thereby respecting the living and the families of those now dead.

gave us a potted life-history but told us nothing of any value for the inquiry.

Suddenly, from getting nowhere, I was given a new and promising lead. The following appeared in the letters column of the paper: 'I was one of the first watchmen employed by Ilford Ltd at Bower House, Havering, and can vouch for such strange happenings as recorded in your article did take place ... the late secretary can confirm the incidents as reported to him by me ....' This initiative was to rescue the case from its dead end. I wrote to him, twice in fact, and what follows emerged from his replies.

Mr H was one of two nightwatchmen taken on by the company in 1948. (I never discovered what had become of the other.) He found Bower House 'rather a formidable place'. It was his job to sit at a table in the hall and every hour to make the rounds, pushing a timing button on each floor and in the basement. The door to Room 13, across from his table, had to be kept securely locked. This had, he thought, a self-closing device, a point of no small importance in the story.

> One morning at 2 a.m. [he wrote], I had just returned from my rounds and sitting at my desk when I heard a slight noise from room 13. I looked over at it and saw it open distinctly, wide enough for a person to get out and the door closed. I went across to this door and looked around room 13 turning on the electric lights, saw nothing, and closed securely the door. I sat at my table rather puzzled how this incident could happen. Suddenly, after about 10 minutes I heard slight footsteps and the door opened again. This time I did feel nervous but went over to the door and closed it securely without looking inside. This happened several times during my employment.
>
> On another occasion at about 4 a.m. I distinctly heard a noise downstairs in the basement in between pressing the button. I thought I should investigate and went to the basement looking in the various rooms but could see nothing suspicious but I also heard noises when sitting at my desk on leaving the basement. So I phoned the Romford police and Mr B the secretary who came from his house. The police made a thorough search of the basement and I think outside but could find nothing which would indicate an entry had been made ....

I must emphasize I never saw any ghostly figure whilst at Bower House but worse continually footsteps used to accompany me on my rounds on various occasions. I think I must have got used to them and noises. But on room 13 door opening I wrote out a full account to Mr B. At no time before my employment with Ilford Ltd was I informed the above house was haunted and emphasize that at no time did I see a ghostly figure.

He later read a book on the house which he borrowed from the library. As to the footsteps, he spoke of them as 'soft'. He added: 'At times I can now remember they stopped and carried on, mostly behind me, mostly coming downstairs or along upstairs passages, but have been in front. I have heard them continue walking after I had sat down in the hall.' But when I asked him if they were confined to any particular area, he replied, 'Yes, mostly in Room 13 and along passage and going upstairs.' The basement sounds were 'rather curious. I have heard a faint tinkling of a row of bells on a wall at the beginning of the basement and footsteps like somebody breaking in .... I got used to them.' By implication, these 'footsteps' must have been loud.

Few could have done better writing some twelve years after these startling incidents. I was struck with the calm tone and restraint of his account. Clear and precise, his recollections bore no trace of embellishment, and he was obviously sincere. Twice he stressed he had seen no ghost. Twice he notes he closed the door securely. The narrative is one of a conscientious man who did his job well. There seems to be no way in which he was prepared or predisposed for what happened.

My next step was clear. My first approach to Ilford Ltd met with a short but courteous rebuff. However, my letter found its way to Mr B, who was happy to see me. He well remembered being called out to Bower House. But in his judgement Mr H was a 'nervous' man. He had been selected for the job by the secretary himself and had not been a watchman before May 1948, when the house was taken over by the company. He had been the only one to report anything unusual, but sadly his original account to Mr B could no longer be traced. Concerning the door to Room 13, the secretary was of the opinion that the self-closing apparatus was probably fitted after the strange behaviour had been reported. Many new locks were found to be necessary as the old ones were 'indifferent'. As for the noises, Mr B spoke of Bower House as 'a house of sounds'. Some stair treads had contracted, resulting in creaks. Some of the windows were loosely fitted, and frequently wind could be heard blowing round the building. The clocking mechanism also made a noise, and the bells in the basement had rusty wires. The house, I was told, bore many signs of subsidence, and I had seen evidence of this for myself in the basement. After his remarks, I knew I had to treat the face value of Mr H's testimony with the greatest caution.

Moreover, there was something else which gave me pause. There would seem to be no reference anywhere, either in books or in the folklore of the district, to any haunting of Bower House before Mr H worked there. Now this is odd indeed if the movements and noises had any association with a long-remote past, although every ghost, I suppose, can choose to start its activities somewhere, selecting its time to bewilder the living. More seriously, though, I think there are good reasons for treating the experience of Mr H and the appearance of 'Lucy' years later as totally separate issues.

In the literature on this subject, a distinction is often made between what are styled primary and secondary effects, it being frequently assumed but only rarely established that the latter are born of the former. Haunts often begin with inexplicable movements and sounds, sometimes of the erratic 'poltergeist' variety. These are then followed at a later stage by transient visual images, which may be generated from within the percipient. Thus a haunted house can turn out to be a haunted mind. Expectation plays its part in this secondary phase, sometimes commencing with the feeling of a presence and sometimes going on to produce a figure. What is difficult in many cases is to determine beyond all ambiguity whether or not the phenomena are purely subjective: 'all in the mind' or a response to something 'out there'.

I think with regard to 'Lucy', not seen before 1959, that we have to assume she was a secondary and generated effect, there being no sure evidence to the contrary. The history of the haunt begins soberly with Mr H. The house then acquires from him a reputation. Individual psychology and the setting in the lonely hours perform the rest. Yet there are one or two pieces which do not fit with ease in the jigsaw. For example, what are we to make of Mr R's dog if the reported details be true? We must all have seen our pets looking intently into space across the room at something which for us is not there. This dog, we are told, had leapt up and gone wild. But a possibility, of course, is that it caught the apprehension of its master.

What, then, can we make of the heart of this matter? What is to be the verdict, yours and mine, on the written testimony of Mr H?

Let us begin with the assertion he was a nervous man. He did admit to feeling anxious the second time the door swung open, after being puzzled when it happened first. But this reads like a perfectly normal reaction, and I am sure many of us would have felt the same. The suggestion, however, is that he was a person with a nervous disposition which led him to misinterpretation. There is a chicken-and-egg problem here. Was he nervous before or after what happened? We have to remember that he claimed to have got used to the sounds in particular, even though he clearly regarded them as strange. Without knowing more about the man, to label him nervous is hardly a starter. 'Nerves' is, in any case, a vague expression, too readily used for dismissal by that so-called common sense which masks a common prejudice.

Coming more to the crux, I see no reason to doubt that the several movements of the door were actual, physical occurrences. There is nothing to indicate that he was in any way conditioned to expect its sudden opening. There is not a hint it was all hallucination. Yet it must be said, he could have been mistaken twelve years later in thinking it was fitted with an automatic closing device. The lock could have been one of those which were suspect. I found the door to be substantial and hanging true. The frame itself showed no sign of distortion.

How could that door have opened without human hand,

'wide enough for a person to get out', and swing back again immediately after? Strained as the hypothesis may seem, it is possible that the movements and the footstep sounds could have been induced by hydraulic action, the effect of underground water exerting a slight, if only momentary, up-lifting pressure on the house. This could, as well, cause the building to act as an amplifier or sounding-board. This geophysical theory has been used with some measure of plausibility to account for certain haunts.

At Bower House, thirty or so yards away from the south-west corner, there is a sixty-foot well to running water. The spot is among bushes and marked by a concrete head with a manhole cover. Through two small apertures in the iron lid, the water could be clearly heard on the day of my visit. I was not able to trace this watercourse, which could be fed through a conduit. There is a lake south-east of the house, about a third of a mile away and downhill. From here a stream winds down to Romford, where it joins the River Rom.

The hypothesis would have to be tested at Bower House by an expert. There is certainly evidence of subsidence, or was when I was there. But this I would stress: the frame of the door to Room 13 showed not the least sign of it. Had the jambs been just a little out of line, I would at once have suspected a defective lock. And *if* it had been self-closing, as Mr H thought, it would indeed have needed a remarkable hydraulic force to move that door inwards. But this was one of those all-important questions never to be settled.

With regard to the sounds heard as footsteps, they are a very common feature of haunted houses. The problem is one of correct identification, and the manner in which we can pattern inanimate noises. Mere likeness, a sound which closely resembles another, is no guarantee of sameness. The 'footsteps' heard by the nightwatchman were mainly slight and soft. They seem to have been noticed by him fairly continuously for much of the time he was there, the best part of a year, and between the hours of two and five in the morning. This is the time when a house is most subject to thermal changes, which can produce contractions in the fabric, especially after a warm day. He may – and I repeat may – have become too familiar with them, thereby reading into them a meaning which was not there. But to set against this, I should think he would have had the nous to tell the difference between a footstep and a common floorboard creak.

It has been a tantalizing tale of 'ifs and buts', as others of the like frequently turn out to be. How I wish I could have been at the foot of those stairs on Mr R's traumatic night, or beside Mr H at his table when that door first moved! Then I could have made my own sightings, notes and observations, fresh with the hour. Such is ever the forlorn hope of the inquisitive outsider, armed with his Hints for Investigating Haunts. But I can take some comfort. Had I been there, no doubt my own state of mind would have become a subject for debate as well.

Not once did I see or talk to a witness. All had to be done by correspondence, one interview and a single daylight visit to the house. I came too late upon the scene, by which time the incident was history. Everything had to be weighed in the balance and was finally found wanting.

And yet there is a coda to the story, adding still more to its strangeness.

Just when I thought my investigation had run its course, I received this note from the newspaper: 'A receptionist knows someone who saw the ghost. She is a friend and should agree to talk.' The lady, who I call here Mrs S, sent me the following short letter in reply to mine:

I thank you for your letter and for your assurance that there is no publicity. There was nothing sensational that I saw at the Bower. Just this, I was on the small landing on the main stairs and looking up saw a man in evening dress i.e. top hat and opera cloak, pass from the room on the left to the room on the right.

This was not alarming in any way for me rather the reverse, he looked charming.

That is all I saw, neither more or less. I hope you will be able to make use of my information.

I elicited further details by taking the risk of sending her a short questionnaire.

She had her experience in the autumn of 1948. The stairs were lit, but she could not recall if the doors in question were open or shut. The figure she saw walked naturally and looked real. It made no sound. The man had a placid face and she judged him to be in his early thirties. He showed no awareness of her. She was about seven feet from the figure and she made no attempt to go into the room after it had done so. At the time of seeing the 'man in evening dress' she was alone, but there were two others elsewhere in the house. When asked what it was that made her feel sure the figure was not a real man, she wrote, 'I had a feeling he was not' – a most subjective answer – and of her reaction to the appearance, said, 'I felt privileged to have seen him.'

Mrs S heard no unusual sounds in the house, where she was an employee of Ilford Ltd, either before or after the date of her experience. However, prior to this she had sensed there was something unusual about the place. I also asked her, 'Had you heard before you saw the ghost that the house was haunted?' and 'Have you ever had a similar experience elsewhere?' To these questions she offered no reply.

There is one point in her account which could be checked. The distance from the landing to the spot where she saw the passing figure *is* about seven feet, as she so correctly remembered.

Her experience is valuable in several respects. It occurred in the very year of that of Mr H, so one could surmise that when she had hers the house had already acquired its reputation for being haunted, gaining currency among the staff if not among outsiders. (I failed to ask Mrs S if she knew Mr H.) In view of the alleged appearances which came years later, it is interesting to find that her ghost was not that of Lucy Baynes, nor could it be said to match the man in the portrait in Room 13, young Lucy's brother.

We are free, of course, to treat the figure seen by Mrs S as purely subjective, vividly imagined and conjured up by her alone. There are but two things I would say. The gentleman with the top hat and the opera cloak bears no relation to anything known about the past occupants of Bower House. Secondly, for her the ghost was clear and lifelike, a far cry from those vague, ill-defined phantoms in long robes which are the products of worry and mystification.

It may well be that there are certain states of mind which trigger events, bringing into perception an order of things normally screened off by our earth-bound senses. But there we must leave the mystery. All, I presume, is quiet at Bower House now, for there has been no news of any further disturbances. The years have closed over its ghosts. They are now a part of that mosaic which is an Essex rich and strange.

Principal Sources

In addition to the main texts consulted, with others too numerous to list below, I have also gone to parish registers, wills and maps (most held at the Essex Record Office) and a variety of old prints and photographs. With regard to localities, I have visited nearly all and have checked out buildings, monuments, inscriptions and the like wherever possible.

The History and Antiquities of the County of Essex, two volumes, Philip Morant (1st ed., 1768)

The History and Topography of the County of Essex, two volumes, Thomas Wright (1831-6)

History, Gazeteer and Directory of the County of Essex, William White (1848)

Kelly's Directories of Essex (particularly for 1933)

The People's History of Essex, D.W. Coller (Meggy & Chalk, Chelmsford. 1861)

The Essex Review: An illustrated Quarterly Record of everything of permanent interest in the County (1892-1957, 65 volumes, printed by Benham & Co, Colchester)

Essex People: 1750-1900, A.F.J. Brown (Essex County Council, Essex Record Office Publications, 1972)

Essex Worthies, Sir William Addison (Phillimore, 1973)

The History of Essex, Elizabeth Ogborne (1814, unfinished)

The Trade Signs of Essex, Miller Christy (Edmund Durrant & Co, Chelmsford, 1887)

Annals of Evangelical Nonconformity in Essex, T.W. Davids (Jackson, Walford & Hodder, London, 1863)

Romantic Essex, Reginald A. Beckett (J.M. Dent & Co, 1st ed. 1901; 2nd ed, 1907)

New Holidays in Essex, ed. Percy Lindley (London, undated, c. 1892)

The Buildings of England: Essex, Nikolaus Pevsner (Penguin Books, 2nd ed., 1965)

The Place-Names of Essex, P.H. Reaney (Cambridge University Press, 1935)

The Life Story of An Essex Lad, Written by Himself, Isaac Mead (A. Driver & Sons, Chelmsford, 1923)

The Essex Village in Days Gone By, Eliza Vaughan (Benham & Co, Colchester, 2nd ed. 1930)

Farnham, Essex, Past and Present, Rev. J.G. Geare (George Allen & Sons, undated, but 1909)

Pleshey: The Village and Retreat House, Margaret Avery (printed by Ellis & Phillips, Bishops Stortford, 3rd ed., 1981)

Fireside Papers: A Countryman's Reflections, Samuel Levy Bensusan (Epworth Press, Edgar C. Barton, London, 1946)

Back of Beyond, S.L. Bensusan (Blandford Press, London, 1945)

Quiet Evening, S.L. Bensusan (Blandford Press, London, 1950)

The Autobiography of Sir John Bramston of Screens in the Hundred of Chelmsford, (Camden Society, 1845)

Forty Years of a Sportsman's Life, Sir Claude Champion de Crespigny, Bart., (Mills & Boon, London, 1910)

Memoirs of Lady Fanshawe (edited, John Lane, The Bodley Head, 1905)

The Diary of Ralph Josselin: 1616-1683, (Camden Society, 1908)

Echoes of the Great War: the Diary of the Rev. Andrew Clark, 1914-1919, edited and with an introduction by James Munson (Oxford University Press, 1985)

Rural England (Vol. I), Rider Haggard (Longmans, Green & Co, 1902)

Aubrey's Brief Lives (Of the modern editions the foremost is that of Oliver Lawson Dick, first published by Martin Secker & Warburg in 1958, and then by Penguin in 1962 and 1972. There is also Richard Barber's, published by the Boydell Press and by Book Club Associates, 1975 and 1982).

The Gentleman's Magazine: various, 1781-1868

The Survey of London by John Stow: 1603 (Everyman edition, J.M. Dent & Sons)

The Dictionary of National Biography

Acknowledgement: I would like to thank Blandford Press, Dorset for allowing me to quote passages from *Quiet Evening* by S.L. Bensusan.

Index of People and Places